Inspirational and Evangelical Short Stories of Faith for Adults

Christian Stahl

© Copyright 2020 by Christian Stahl - All rights reserved

License Notice

This document is geared towards providing exact and reliable information in regards to the topic and issue covered. In no way is it legal to reproduce, duplicate, download, or transmit any part of this document in either electronic means or in printed format without the consent of the author or publisher. Recording of this publication is strictly prohibited and any storage of this document is not allowed unless with written permission from the publisher.

All rights reserved

The information provided herein is stated to be truthful and consistent, in that any liability, in terms of inattention or otherwise, by any usage or abuse of any policies, processes, or directions contained within is the solitary and utter responsibility of the recipient reader. Under no circumstances will any legal responsibility or blame be held against the publisher or author for any reparation, damages, or monetary loss due to the information herein, either directly or indirectly. The information herein is offered for informational purposes solely, and is universal as so. Any name and content in this book is fiction and not related to any real events or persons. The presentation of the information is without contract or any type of guarantee assurance.

Details of all the author's available books and upcoming titles can be found at:
www.shortstoycollections.com

Foreword	4
The Busy CEO	7
The Girl and the Note	11
The Man of My Dreams	20
Living Alone in Modern Times	26
Almost in Paradise	30
The Law Instructor of Jericho	38
Living in Nature	43
The Incredulous Psychiatrist	51
The Girl from the Salvation Army	56
The Loving Husband	66
The Evil Double Life	72
The Dying Veteran	91
The Old Bridge	95
The True Story of Friar Max Kolbe	99
The Emperor's Gifts	102
Puppies for Sale	105
The Future Kingdom of Peace	108
The Horseman	118
The Major	123
A Strange Dream	127
The Boulder	134
The Preacher and the Atheist	137
Our Old Town When Times Were Bad and Money Scarce	139
God's Wonderful Way	143
The True Story of the Evangelist Richard Baxter	143
I Met Her in the Opera	147
The Painter	153
Cafe Lisbon	159
The London Marathon	167
Endless Love on a Dream Vacation	174
My Name is Lazarus - A Classic Tale	179
Different Heavens According to Peter	199

30 Inspirational and Evangelical Short Stories of Faith for Adults

Foreword

This book is devoted to all who appreciate Christian stories and faith narrative. This collection of 35 short stories includes modern as well as classical tales, all written to inspire and give hope to those who are suffering. The spirit of help, hope and faith can be found everywhere and can be instilled in anyone throughout their life. Learning about faith is the first step towards using it as guidance in all real-life circumstances. Jesus shows himself to those who are seeking his guidance, spirit and manifestation in their own way; it is the stories that have been accumulated for 2000 years that help people achieve this spirit.

Mostly humour centered, some with historical backgrounds related to classic tales, and a few based on real historical events, this international collection of short stories will leave the reader entertained and inspired. The collection also contains a selection of true short stories, like the retelling of friar Max Kolbe and the old tale of Lazarus. The collection is also an attempt to take inspiration from classic Christian events, resulting in an execution of biblical approaches in modern stories adapted to the current times. As a whole the book provides a teaching of faith that is informative while also remaining light-hearted with the use of comedic elements.

The Busy CEO

A young and successful manager drove his Jaguar a little too fast through a suburban street. He was on the watch out for children who might run into the street between the cars parked along the side of the road. He reduced his speed when he thought he noticed movement. However, when his car passed the spot in question, no child appeared. Instead, a brick crashed into the Jaguar's driver's door! He screeched to a stop and reversed the Jaguar to where the brick had been thrown.

The angry driver jumped out of the car, grabbed the first child he saw there, pushed him against a parked car and yelled, "What were you thinking and who are you? What on earth is this? This is a brand new car and that brick you just threw there will cost you a lot of money. Why did you do that?"

The little boy said apologetically, "Please, Mr... please, I'm sorry, but I didn't know what else to do. I threw the stone because nobody else would stop..."

As tears ran down his face and dripped from his chin, the boy pointed to a spot behind a parked car. "That's my brother," he said. "He rolled over the curb and fell out of his wheelchair, and I can't pick him up on my own." Meanwhile, the boy, sobbing heavily, asked the astonished manager, "Could you please help me put him back in his wheelchair? He's injured, and he's too heavy for me to carry."

Deeply moved, the driver tried to swallow the lump that was rapidly rising in his throat. He immediately lifted the disabled boy back into his wheelchair and then pulled out a linen handkerchief to dab off the fresh scratches and cuts. A quick glance told him that everything would soon be fine.

"Thank you, and God bless you," said the grateful child to the stranger.

Too shaken for words, the man simply watched as the boy pushed his wheelchair-bound brother down the sidewalk.

It was a long, slow walk back to his Jaguar. The damage was clearly visible. However, the driver never had the dented side door repaired. He left the dent there as a constant reminder of its message.

Don't rush through life so fast that someone has to throw a brick at you to get your attention!

God whispers to our soul and speaks to our heart. Sometimes, when we don't have time to listen, he has to throw a brick at us. It's our choice whether we listen or not.

The Girl and the Note

I feel the wind brushing past the tip of my nose and try to concentrate on my breathing. A few seconds later, I feel better and even a bit cooler. The breathing exercise has, it seems, also reduced my sweating, and now I can enjoy my surroundings even more. I sit on the park bench under a big, shady chestnut tree and enjoy every little breeze that blows around my ears on this warm summery day.

Our village is located in a rural Christian community where there are still old statues in parks and occasional crosses in front of the church and a few houses.

What a different environment this is from my workplace in the nearby town where I work part-time in a cubic office as a customer service representative.

It feels great sitting under the trees, the birds are singing, and I have traded headphones and long pants for a t-shirt and Bermuda shorts... I deserve time out to relax in nature.

While my gaze wanders, I notice a little girl on the other side of the park path. She looks sad and is wearing strange, old-fashioned braids. The two braids hang heavily over her shoulders.

She comes closer and seems not to notice anyone around her.

As she passes me, I hear a whisper, but can hardly understand what she is saying. It sounds like she's practising an apology under her breath.

I wonder if she had trouble at school and is now dragging herself grudgingly home. Or maybe she had a fight with a schoolmate... and now she's sorry.

My gaze follows the girl, and suddenly I notice that an old man has sat down on the bench next to me.

"Good afternoon," he greets me in a friendly way. His face is very appealing.

He leans his walking stick against the trash can next to the bench and folds his rough hands without adding another word.

For minutes, only the rustling leaves of the gnarled tree can be heard, accompanied by the chirping of the birds.

Strange, the little girl kneels to pray before an old wooden cross which I had never noticed before in this park,... and the man next to me is praying as if the world around him did not exist.

The silence is eerie, as is the situation, and I'm sitting right in the middle of it.

"Her name's Barbara," my bench mate says in a croaky voice.

"Do you know that girl?"

"Yes and no, but if you wish, I'd be happy to tell you our story. However, now I have to go over there and do my job."

With a smile, the old man leans on the stick and shuffles, step by step over to the inconspicuous wooden cross. No doubt people no longer notice it except the man and the girl, although hundreds of people pass by every day.

The girl, Barbara, has already left when the old man bends to the ground in pain and seems to pick up something.

How weird.

Curiosity gets the better of me, and I want to hear the old man's reasons. He turns around and is approaching me again.

With a groan of exhaustion, he sits down and is holding a handful of colorful pieces of paper.

Again his shaky fingers fold up tightly after reading the child's handwriting. While he prays, he presses the little pieces of paper in his palm.

"We don't know each other personally, but we do have someone in common," the old man finally says. "During the summer months, I occasionally work in the city, and I was out and about here in the village park collecting the garbage, which the occasional day tourist leaves around. You have to know that my wife Linda died a short time ago ... it was hard to say goodbye, even if it probably won't be long before we see each other again..."

The old man breathes heavily, pauses for a moment.

"See, we are believers, and won't be separated for long, as I too will go home to my Lord rather sooner than later. Anyway, I've had a lot of grief recently."

He pauses, almost seems to fall asleep and then continues. "Often, in the evenings, when my work was done, I used to sit here on this bench, looking for peace, comfort and meaning. I could no longer bear staying at home where it was quiet and lonely without my Linda. For forty-seven years, we shared every moment, the good and the dark times, but together we had each other and our faith.

On one of these last evenings, I felt especially sad, because it was Linda's birthday. So, I sat here and asked God to help me with my grief. I also requested to be allowed to come to him soon. But then Barbara came. She cried, sobbed so loudly I thought a catastrophe of some sort had happened to her. I could truly feel her pain, her desperate grief, although, at that time, I did not know what the reason was. I needed a moment of silence. I closed my eyes for a few seconds and asked God what I could do for these two suffering beings, and then, it hit me, I knew. I had suddenly found a task I would carry out from then on. However, I didn't speak to the girl because I didn't want to scare her. I was and am a stranger to her. But I tried to show her how Jesus listens to her prayers and how undeniably he loves her."

He turns around to look at me with eyes full of sadness. "Since that night, she and I have been here about the same time every day."

"What does she write on the colored pieces of paper? I don't quite understand."

My old bench neighbor smiles at me and lays his hand on mine before he starts to explain.

"Yes, there's a lot you can't understand right away. You're still young...but let me tell you, on these notes Barbara writes down everything that concerns her. Her fears, her worries, her mistakes and the quarrels she has with other children. So, when Barbara took off, she left the notes on the cross after a prayer, and I later picked them up. Seeing these notes took all her worries away. In a way, she knew about Jesus and had asked Him for help, guidance and sometimes for forgiveness. Those notes seemed childish, but her faith was real, her hope in Jesus paid off because she came here with all her worries and left them here in the park. But there is something more. Since that evening, I take the little one into my prayers. Sometimes we even pray together and yet each in our way even though we are only a few metres apart. We both pray to him who forgives guilt, dries tears and gives joy."

While I ponder in amazement and try to fathom what I have heard, the old man offers a mysterious smile.

"Barbara still comes here often and does the same thing, because who can say today, at this time, if life will be easy?

Sometimes, when she walks, she smiles and hops like a bird that has just lost its load and has learned to fly again...and you, young friend, do you know who helps them?"

Without one more word, he pulls a purple note out of his jacket pocket and writes in shaky letters,

All the guilt is Jesus. For you, you are free. For I have loved you forever and ever' says God to you.

He drags himself slowly back to the cross, puts the note under a stone and says goodbye with a friendly smile as he walks past the bench once more.

The Man of My Dreams

It was an ordinary morning. Almost compulsively, through a rather long habit, she started the day with a thought of helping others, followed by a short prayer.

Everything was going, as usual, that day. she experienced no creeping depressions, no unforeseen, emerging joy, nothing unusual. No lottery wins, no promotion, no bad news, such as the sentence, *Cancer, have you heard?*

Everything was going along fine until he entered her house. She asked him to sit in the living room, but he wanted to sit in the kitchen. She was not prepared for visitors, so it took a little while before she got used to his presence.

He was in no hurry. His eyes, his ears, his heart rested. The silence seemed familiar to him. Then he began to speak the words her spirit had hungered and thirsted for so many years.

"You know, I love looking at you. And honestly, you smell like heaven, I feel like your future home when I'm near you. I enjoy your presence so much."

She got scared, but then she sucked in his words deep inside. Had the stranger sought and found her hidden, secret desires? How did he know her longings? Her heart burned. She looked at him. He looked at her. *How beautiful he is*, she thought and was immediately ashamed.

"How beautiful you are," she heard him say. "I see the veil of my presence over you. Grace and peace cover your head. It's so delicious to my eyes, I'm happy just to be near you."

She listened. Time passed. When she looked up again, she was overcome by a quiet trembling.

I must never again let these words slip from my mind. Never again. I need them so much. I was starving. I was thirsty. I must write these words down in my book, my book of life.

The kitchen was filled with warmth and pleasure. Forgotten was the mountain of unwashed dishes and the dark tiles waiting for a broom. Nor was her very special problem, which she struggled with at regular intervals, of any interest. Or was it?

Suddenly she got up to get her booklet, which she kept carefully hidden from everyone. No one was allowed to look inside.

"When I am gone," she had once declared to her children, "you may look in the book. Not before."

Why did she feel the need to reveal her innermost self to the stranger in her kitchen? Although she was somehow wondering, her mind knew exactly why she did. The unread pages of her life drove her to do it. Her extraordinary guest was to teach her. He would be able to. Who else?

She picked up her book, blew the dust off the cover and opened it. Slowly she turned back the pages.

"Childhood," she read her own writing out loud and looked up.

Where was the stranger? Was he still there? Of course, he was. It seemed to her that he was waiting for this very moment. He had all the time in the world.

No, I have to hurry... This, and that need to be done immediately.

"Let go," he encouraged her after several minutes.

"Why?" she blurted out. "Where have you been? Are you not pure love? Couldn't you have intervened? Protected me back then? Everything would have been very different in my life. Very different."

"Go on," he encouraged.

All her misery broke loose. She gave vent to her anger with accusations. Between breathless moments she made sure he was still there. How could he endure it? Why did he not leave? Oh no, now she was crying too. In front of a strange man. Why didn't he leave?

"Go on," he encouraged her. "Keep talking, please!"

Nothing was going as it was meant to that day. Nothing at all. Everything was extraordinary. They looked into each other's eyes.

"Period," she said all of a sudden, out of the blue.

He was not at all surprised at the abrupt ending of the conversation. He took her book of life in his hands, asked for a pen and began to write in it. After a while, he put both aside and spoke.

"Give me your misery again and again and again. Give me all your complaints. Pour out your heart to me every day. Beloved, my food is to do my Father's will. His will is to do good to you. If I carry out his will, my soul will be satisfied. Beloved bride, only you can feed me. So feed me! Give me to drink! You satisfy my hunger with your presence. You will quench my thirst when we have true fellowship. Do not let me hunger; do not let me thirst. Open up your heart. This is the will of my Father in heaven who sent me to you. His will I do gladly. I always want to further his work, even in you."

Living Alone in Modern Times

You're home alone. Everyone's out except you. You work for hours, first in the office, then from home, often even in your kitchen.

You are probably the only one. This is an inevitable fact, or better fate if you believe in it. The truth is you often find life dull and boring. Day in, day out, the same thing, just working on the computer, cleaning, doing the laundry, commitments, ordering food, and civic restrictions don't make your life any easier either. And yet you too long for a full life, want to bite into it, taste and feel it.

Yes, sometimes you envy strangers who seem to lead such a full life, apparently without obligations. How would you like to escape? Somewhere where there is abundance, where life is vibrant.

"Wait," I hear a voice from somewhere, "and what about me? Am I not your best friend in the world? I promised to be with you. And I am. I'm with you all the time, in your house, doing all your housework. But you hardly take any notice of me, you treat me like a stranger, like a guest who may drop in on you from time to time. Do you know how that makes me feel? My presence doesn't seem enough for you. It hurts my feelings. Am I a bore for you? You never say a word to me, though I pine for every word from your lips. It has to be said at least once. All of it. Of me. How else could we have a personal relationship? Don't you know who I am? I don't know a single person you hold in such contempt as you do me. Everyone else is more important to you. Do you seek recognition and appreciation from people? What do they think of me? What are they saying? What about me? I'm the only help you have. And you know it. Where you go, I go. I'm always a few steps ahead of you, far enough so that you and I can make eye contact. Always, assuming you want me to be in your line of sight, for I rarely am. Are you disappointed in me? I wish I could guide, guide and protect you better. But you won't let me. When push comes to shove, then, yes, you call me. Once I have helped you, you leave, often without thanking me. Isn't it I who'll take you all the way? Or do you mean to find your way alone? Not a single person in the whole world can find the way home, no matter how smart they think they are. No one on your great globe. Does that annoy you? You are so precious to me. I love you so much. I've given my whole life for our future together. Right now, I'm taking care of your place in heaven. I know all your desires and preferences. I'm totally committed to them and more. Much, much more.

    Day and night, I dream of a life together with you. Can't you see that? I envy you. I want to pull you to me through everything that happens to you, even if your ears are clogged, and you prefer your ways. When we're closer, your soul will be healed. That's why I can't leave you alone. I can't give you up. You'd be lost without me. That's why I'm knocking at your heart's door. I look forward to it every time you open up to me, to the time we spend together, to the time we share...Do you want to think about all this?"

Almost in Paradise

The sun had almost disappeared from the horizon, only a few last rays beautified the sky. At this stage of the sunset, there were usually more applicants asking for entry into Paradise.

It was one of the countless evenings the cherub Haziel had spent at the entrance to Paradise for thousands of years.

After dark, he had to be especially careful. It was the hour of the supposedly very clever ones who tried to slip into Paradise unnoticed. The rush had decreased noticeably in recent years, many people were busy in their daily, all-consuming hardship, and people were taking more than the essential in times of need. During their lifetime, most of the inhabitants of the earth had other paradises in mind, which usually had something to do with ego, human passions and especially with material things.

In addition, the type of people seeking admission had changed. At the moment, it was mainly people who had killed themselves and believed that only honey, wine and a flock of virgins would sweeten their days in Paradise. They were at the wrong address with him. After all, Paradise was not a place for the dead, since there were the seven heavens and Abraham's womb.

But again and again, the dead tried to enter it, even those who should have known better. Were the aspirants not marked with small triangular symbols on their chests in the color that determined their temporary future? Thanks to this element, Haziel knew right away which of the streets he had to send them to. This was a simple matter, as these also had color markings.

He had often racked his brains over the meaning of colors. Red was no doubt the hellfire. But what did the other colors mean? For those who were marked green, there might have been hope. He assumed that the yellow and blue were probably not Christian, but nevertheless, believers in God. White was the most mysterious. He could only imagine the sky. However, the Scriptures stated that the final entry into the eternal Paradise would only take place at the end of the world.

There, these souls might stay in an intermediate place. But what about those who had already been canonized?

The Scriptures spoke of one hundred and forty-four thousand who were once allowed to look at God. He had not counted those who had strayed here, but it seemed to him that there were already more who had arrived with the white mark. There had to be more because in the Scriptures only the children of Israel were counted in this number.

It was still unclear whether those who had not yet been purified, perhaps those who were not marked in white, were among them.

Haziel often wondered about the purpose of Paradise. He always stood in the same place at the entrance, armed with a fiery sword, and was not allowed to move an inch. At first, a second cherub had stood by his side. When the child was born in Bethlehem, he was allowed to float away to sing at his birth. The cherub had not come back.

From his position, Haziel could see into Paradise. It was always the same picture. Beautiful flowers, magnificent looking animals and to his delight the singing of the birds. But he never saw a human being. Hadn't the criminal been promised on the cross to come to Paradise the very same day? Even *he* never passed by here. Besides, Jesus said in the Scriptures, 'And was carried up to heaven'.

What was so special about this place? It was more of a place for the living because the dead no longer needed all this abundance of fruit. Or did the souls want back what was once meant for them? They had probably forgotten that nothing lasts forever, and many had gambled it away. There was also a passage in the Scriptures in which there was talk of a new heaven and a new earth. If that were to happen, then this Paradise would actually be superfluous.

Haziel kept getting sidetracked. Not only the rustling in the nearby bushes, which came from a hare but also his heretical thoughts were the cause. These came from boredom. His original task was to sing. Together with his brothers, he had not only pleased the Creator, but also the whole of heaven. Then he was assigned this task. No more singing. He had not even thought of complaining. Too fresh was the memory of the banishment of Lucifer, that radiant angel who stood in such a high place and yet still wanted more. No, he was not like that, not Haziel. I'd rather stand guard here than be an outcast.

Nevertheless, he would have liked to have done something else. Should he dare to try and see if his voice was still as good and strong? Maybe that would help against frustration. Was that even allowed? It had not been forbidden to him. Courageously he tried a tone. Nothing, not a single sound! Yes, there was something. But it did not come from him. It was a faint cry.

Right in front of him lay a dead little child. How had it gotten there? Had he overlooked it while he was dealing with his own problems? Children rarely came to this place. In fact, their souls were taken by an angel after their death. Where they were taken to, Haziel didn't know. Anyway, he had to act. He searched for the mark on the body. It was red. "No," he cried, "it can't be!"

He wiped and wiped at the paint. Finally, it faded until pure white was visible. Blood had run over the mark and dried. He picked up the child and carried him to the crossroads. There, an angel stood ready and took the child with him.

Frightened, Haziel fled back. He had left his post without thinking. But his fiery sword was still there and had taken over his task.

Every time it was a child, Haziel was disgusted with his work. He knew that it was not for him to criticize the Lord's actions. However, some decisions were unfathomable. Was it possible that over time he had become accustomed to the way of thinking of people who questioned everything and anything? He had to change that, for he was after all a cherubim and obliged to his Lord. He had almost fallen for the whispers of this Beelzebub. He was clever, extremely clever! He knew all his victims' weak points. And he was probably bored.

Haziel did not consider that night a good one. More and more, he longed for the end of the world. Perhaps in the next eternity, he would be given a better task. Was that a new temptation? This Lucifer was persistent, after all, he had even tried with the Son of God. So, better resist these whispers, not complain, but continue, without brooding, and believe, just believe, because this occupation certainly had a purpose.

The Law Instructor of Jericho

Jesus had been teaching in the temple for several days. Some of his listeners were impressed by his teaching, others took offense. Among them was a law instructor who wanted to provoke Jesus by asking him how he could attain the Kingdom of Heaven.

On one side of the temple, Maheli, a Levite, had taken care of the lampstands entrusted to him. At first, he only heard excerpts of the conversation between Jesus and the law instructor. Shocked, he listened carefully when he heard a story that was familiar to him. How did this Jesus know about it?

It was about a man who had been attacked on the way from Jericho to Jerusalem. Neither a Levite nor a priest who passed by had taken care of him, though he was lying on the ground. He also overheard that a Samaritan had helped this man. This act was praised by Jesus. After all, every person is obliged to love his neighbor, and this love leads to the Kingdom of Heaven.

Maheli knew this road. He had walked it many times before and knew that there was a lot of danger lurking on this stretch of approximately thirty kilometers. The area was unsettling and deserted, with no houses, only bushes and rocks. Many travellers were attacked, and Maheli had seen many victims lying there.

This speech about Jesus made him angry.

What was the itinerant preacher thinking? If he knew the Scriptures so well, he must also know about the Purity Laws. The assaulted victim lying before Maheli was suffering from severe blood loss. It looked as if life had long since drained out of him. Maheli should have touched him to make sure he was dead. If that were the case, he would not be allowed to do temple service for seven days.

Furthermore, he would have to submit to several cleaning regulations. Besides, in what way could he have helped the wounded man? His water receptacle was almost empty. He had only gone halfway, and there was no well from which he could refill it. There was no oil or wine in his luggage, and no other hiker for miles around. Finally, the priest who had been spoken of had also gone on without taking care of the man. For he too, was aware of the consequences of such an intervention.

Maheli felt restless. Again and again, he heard the subliminal accusation that Jesus had made against the assailant for refusing to help the victim. Until to now, he had regarded his profession of service in the temple as his most important task. Had not God Himself called the tribe of the Levites to the service? He had generously forgiven them for the attack on Shechem by the ancestors Simeon and Levi. However, Jacob had refused to bless them. Had he, Maheli, acted wrongfully? In what way could he have helped the poor man?

Suddenly he felt a faint movement of air. Was this the good spirit who had appeared to him before? Maheli did not know exactly who he was, but he suspected that it was one of the angels who worked to help people. Although Maheli was prepared for this, he was startled when a voice spoke to him.

"Fear not, no evil will befall you. I know you're plagued with doubt because you didn't take care of that poor man. Although you are right to assume that you lacked the means to effectively help. On the other hand, put yourself in his shoes. What could you have done for him?"

Maheli replied hesitantly, "I could have sat with him and calmed him down until help arrived."

"You see, it's not hard after all. It's not always about big deeds. The willingness to help alone has many faces. By the way, Jesus equates the commandment 'to love one's neighbor' with faith in a higher power. I hope you will act differently next time."

Maheli breathed a weak, "Thank you, I promise." And he was serious. "Charity and my faith in a higher power belong together, they cannot be separated," he murmured.

Finally, he fell into a restful sleep.

Living in Nature

My husband and I decided years ago to live in the country. A lot of things led to that decision back then, but that was a long time ago now, and on this quiet morning, I started the day by taking a short walk into the nearby forest.

Of course, I always need a few minutes to understand and really experience this small change from our simple dwelling to the gentle nature.

The footpath started outside our property, where the path narrowed down, surrounded by dense bushes and tall trees. If I hadn't known better, I might have thought I was lost in the wilderness.

And there it stood, a tall spruce at the edge of the clearing. In this neighborhood, there were others like it, as well as other types of trees of all sizes. Together they painted a beautiful picture, especially shortly after sunrise, when the dew still glittered freshly on the needles and leaves. The blackbirds that had sung to themselves a little earlier were accompanied by other chamber singers, and the first mosquitoes began circling around the tips of the branches.

At the foot of the spruce, the ants had created a mighty hill in the last few weeks. A few steps further into the clearing, in an old dead tree trunk surrounded by delicate purple Bellflowers, the small swarm of hornets had by now developed into a real state and were using the narrow forest path that ran by the spruce as their main flight route.

Only yesterday a pair of Pine Warblers had accepted the wide-spreading branches of the spruce as a welcome invitation to build a well-protected nest high up in its branches.

If nothing extraordinary happened, this would considerably increase in size in the coming years due to its construction.

Usually, one could feel pure life here on all floors — under, between and above the forest trees. This was why hikers and even hunters paused reverently again and again. They would close their eyes, breath in deeply and relax, as they tried to capture this precious moment deep into their hearts for eternity. They could then feed on this magical experience again with closed eyes in the hectic everyday life.

One rainy evening a dragonfly appeared between the dripping branches. On its flight home to the nearby pond, it had been surprised by the rain and had sought shelter under the broad branches for a while.

It started bragging about one of its last trips to the nearby outskirts of the city, leaving those in the audience who knew nothing about it in open amazement. Yes, the dragonfly had also seen a fir tree there. However, this one had been much more colorful, standing alone, as crowds of dancing and celebrating people had surrounded it. Yes, white and blue ribbons with flags and garlands had hung down from its proud branches, it was simply indescribable. It was indeed stately and imposing to look at. The tree was so radiantly beautiful that another dragonfly almost flew into a light pole. Moreover, people would always put up new trees of this kind, which they had previously carefully selected in the forest.

To be such a magnificent tree once in a lifetime would finally be something meaningful, thought the spruce, given all that the dragonfly had said. No longer to be one of many trees living day after day half-hidden here at the edge of the forest, having to live such a bounded existence. Colorful ribbons instead of bird droppings, garlands instead of swarms of mosquitoes and dancing children instead of dead caterpillars and beetles and ants. Yes, this must be the true fulfillment for every tree, absolutely!

Deep inside, the tree had been asking itself for a long time, what the meaning of its existence could be and also if it were possible to step out of the shadow of the other trees and realize itself in a different way.

Time can pass more slowly in the country, it seems. I remember last autumn, which came a few days later, bringing a firework of reds and yellows to the clearing, as well as the countless leaves and fruits.

However, when winter came with its mass of snow taking a few branches from the tree, the desire of last summer became so overwhelming that I almost overlooked the first anemones in early March. These greeted the onsets of spring, between the now snow-free foliage and a thick layer of needles.

But even the warming rays of the sun, the bees busily flying around in the pastures as well as the butterflies dancing above the sky could no longer fill the emptiness that was like a constant and desolate companion.

One morning a loud roar could be heard from afar, followed by its smell. A small group of cheerful men with ropes and chains followed the exhaust clouds of a tractor. I only recognized the strange-looking object in the back of the tractor at the last moment. It was a chainsaw.

What could they be doing with that machine out here at such an early hour?

Still absorbed in these considerations, I noticed that the group of workers had come to a halt right in front of the large spruce tree. One of the men pointed directly at it and at its mighty trunk, whereupon all the others nodded in agreement.

We watched the massacre from a distance, at least what we could see of it.

After they had removed the spruce, we saw the heron's nest hanging destroyed in the neighboring tree, and the anthill totally trampled. Not only did the pair of herons have to build a new nest on such short notice but the smaller trees were left without shelter.

They were now fully exposed to the wind and rain and would grow more slowly and bent by the elements.

My husband told me that I was too sensitive. He also taught me that nature is just constant adaptation, it is creative, explosive in its power and full of life energy, and regenerates itself. He also told me that this principle should apply to people and that we should always make the best of things. The main thing is that we are happy.

In any case, I never saw the workers again, and where the old stump stood, hundreds of small fresh shrubs, mushrooms and young flower stems blossomed — the old wood had come to life once more.

My husband died last month, and since we lived alone, I buried him in a secret place in the forest, not far from the old spruce, where a small gentle mound of earth, which I shoveled by myself, still stood and was now blooming in March like a small natural paradise. There was no other place that could boast small flowers and blades of grass as juicy as on the unrecognizable heap of earth.

Since I know how beautiful the blooming is in this place, I sit here more often and enjoy nature. Sometimes, between the branches and leaves, a light appears. From a certain distance, it resembles a translucent figure wearing a type of white cape. I sometimes think I even recognize the face of a man who knows me and smiles.

The Incredulous Psychiatrist

Ingo and his sister Stefanie live in a little Catholic town in South Germany. Ingo is twelve years old, and Stefanie is one year younger. They are both intelligent children with very modern views and love to play on the Internet. They are also passionate video gamers and love posting on social media networks. Their parents are both educationists. Their father works in the hospital, and their mother is independent and has her own small psychiatric office.

It is Christmas time, and Christmas songs are blasting out from the shops and supermarkets, setting the scene for the excitement of the unwrapping of presents and family fun.

Although the siblings are conservatively educated, they don't particularly like Christmas. In the last few years, when distant relatives came to visit, there were a lot of arguments.

Last weekend, on a Catholic holiday, one of their father's colleagues also came to stay, and a dispute started about church or religion. This was a clear sign that they were no longer going to put up with their parents' religious ideas.

When the siblings found out that their parents intended to go to the Christmas service in the church, they complained bitterly.

Being as intelligent as they were, the siblings underlined the fact that the family never usually went to church, and this was therefore totally unfair. However, their mother pointed out that in small towns, there was often a fair amount of gossiping, and it would be a good idea to adapt to the local traditions. Furthermore, it would also show the neighbors that they were good and charitable people, as they had to preserve a certain image in the town.

Stefanie and Ingo had a different opinion.

At Christmas, the siblings insisted on staying at home. Ingo preferred to participate in a live game on the Internet, and Stefanie was busy on Facebook and Instagram.

This, of course, led to a dispute, and both parents blamed the children for being poorly educated and lacking good manners. Ironically, it never crossed their minds that they were the ones who had educated the two children.

The argument went on for a while until the parents decided they needed to talk among adults about the dispute.

What were they supposed to do? Should they force the siblings to go to church, or was there another solution to the problem?

The mother suddenly came up with a bright idea and suggested they meet up with the other psychiatrists at the office to analyze the situation with her colleagues.

After a few calls, they planned to meet in the evening with a small group of pedagogues and psychiatrists to exchange their opinions on the subject.

However, this experience proved to be an unexpectedly enlightening one for both of them.

When the parents returned from their meeting with the experts, Ingo and Stefanie were in for a surprise. Their parents announced that they had reached a decision and that no one had to go to church that year.

"Why have you suddenly changed your minds?" asked Stefanie, curious to know what had led to this welcomed decision.

"Well, during the meeting, my colleagues put *us* under scrutiny. As it turns out, we both have problems regarding religion. It seems that we are a little too religious and that after all, religion is considered as a type of mental illness," answered the mother.

The Girl from the Salvation Army

Of course, the eighties were the best in old Berlin, as far as I remember. At that time Berlin was still a divided city, flourishing economically and sinking into the mire at the same time. But it was also the time of personal freedom, of openness, perhaps even of free love.

I remember that stupid hat that sat on top of her braided dark blond hair was the first thing I noticed about Iris. And the dark-blue uniform she came up to me in. Of course, I didn't know her name was Iris at the time. She was holding a sheet of paper with the lurid title *War Cry*.

"What *are you* selling?" she wanted to know.

I held up the well-known street magazine that I had been selling around the central station for two years.

She smiled. "Wanna swap?"

I shook my head. "Sorry, I make my living selling this paper. Of the sixty-one people who pay for it, I get 50 pennies, and I need those pennies badly as a welfare recipient."

I held out the cards to her. She nodded and reached into her pocket that contained a whole stack of her newspaper. She pulled out a wallet and gave me a two-coin. "Keep the change."

Then she handed me her paper. "But don't throw it away. Read it. Bye."

I watched her as she walked on.

Suddenly she turned around again and smiled. "Jesus loves you!"

Jesus loves you. Sure, I thought, of course. That's why I've been doing so well for the last five years. First my divorce, then the work-accident with the complicated fracture and eight weeks later my expulsion from Meyers Construction, the company for which I was employed for almost five years with the most dangerous renovation work in the still very much in-need-of-renovation West Berlin.

"We are sorry, but with a serious injury like yours, which will never really heal properly, even if you only work for the company as a driver, you will no doubt be required to help with the loading." That was it.

I no longer had an apartment of my own either, instead, I shared a flat with three other men. I had fifteen square meters to myself. We shared the kitchen and a bathroom. *But Jesus loves you, of course.* Nice, but that girl was a bit unworldly

When in the evening, I had counted the takings and made myself comfortable on my old but cozy couch with a bottle of beer, I grabbed the *War Cry* and leafed through it. At that moment the scales fell from my eyes, as they say. That girl was in the Salvation Army! I had only moved to Berlin three months earlier, so I had not yet come into contact with these people.

I couldn't help smiling. If I happened to meet the young woman again, I would ask her some really good questions. I was good at that. In Berlin, I had made a preacher sweat once.

The opportunity presented itself a week later when I saw the little 'Soldier of Christ' — one of three million worldwide according to the *War Cry* — again on the cow dam in front of the department store. This time, however, she was not alone. She was singing a pious song together with some other uniformed men who accompanied her with a guitar. After the last verse, Iris broke away from the small troop and came towards me. She handed me a flyer.

"If you feel like it, come by our place sometime. We have a service at a quarter past eight and after that our coffee bar opens. My name is Iris, by the way."

Iris, a powerful Greek name, flashed through my mind. I couldn't help smiling.

She raised an eyebrow. "What's so funny?"

"Oh, nothing," I replied and introduced myself as well.

"Peter Schmidt. Where can I find your club?"

'Jesus lives in the Bahnhof Zoo', was written on the large sign above the entrance of the old station vaults, where the Salvation Army had its headquarters. This is how I had read it in the *War Cry*. I had missed the service — Iris, seemed a little disappointed about it — but I never say no to a cup of coffee. And the coffee bar, which quickly filled with men and women, was a really cozy place.

"Say, Max..." Iris poured herself a cup of coffee.

Ah, and now the first attempt of conversion was probably coming. Nothing. Instead, that night we talked about everything but God. Strange. Wasn't that the point of the invitation? Okay, at one point Iris briefly touched on the subject when she talked about her work and about what the Salvation Army did — from caring for the elderly in need of care and giving out food and clothing to advising debtors to helping addicts. I must admit I was impressed.

"And why are you doing all this?" was what I wanted to know from Iris. That was my first mistake.

"Because I have seen that God loves me." She smiled. "And now I just want to pass on some of that love. Very practical. There are enough people out there who just talk about it. What I like about the Salvation Army is that they do something about the need. That's why I'm here."

Well, I had no objection to that. Instead, that night I felt something I hadn't felt in ten years. I was in love.

When we said goodbye, I asked Iris if we could see each other again soon.

"You mean here?"

I shook my head. "I was actually thinking about taking a walk after work. Maybe one of these parks around here."

She hesitated.

"Or do you have a boyfriend?"

"No, that's not it. But I don't actually do this sort of thing."

I wasn't ready to give up that easily. "You invited me for coffee, now I'd like to return the favor with a bratwurst or a chicken sandwich!"

She smiled. "Chicken sandwich sounds good."

"Saturday afternoon?"

She nodded. "But only until seven. Then I've got to be back at the station entrance with another Salvation Army man, to hand out papers."

Iris works in Berlin's most wicked train station, behind every corner, there were johns, prostitutes and sex shops, and there were drunks in every corner. A strange place to work. If someone had told me that...

On Saturday, we met at Bahnhof Zoo, and from there we took a two-hour walk towards the zoo. We enjoyed the wonderful summer weather and talked about everything. Time flew by and when we said goodbye to each other, we each knew each other's life story, favorite music and favorite food! By the way, today was the first time Iris had given up her uniform, and I liked her even more.

When we shook hands — I would have much rather kissed her — she suddenly said, "You could actually accompany me this evening. Or do you have other plans?"

I shook my head. "Not really, but is that even possible? I don't belong to your club, after all."

"Oh, that's all right." She smiled. "I'll be right there with you."

So that Saturday night, I went up and down the cow's perineum with Iris, and Herbert, an older man. I had definitely fallen in love with this young woman, who had only entered my life a few days earlier. My admiration for Iris grew from hour to hour.

Even though not everyone to whom she offered her newspaper was happy to accept it or engage in conversation, Iris remained friendly. There had to be something to her faith, after all.

Just before midnight, all the newspapers were distributed, and I was dog-tired.

"Will you join me for a glass of juice or something?" I asked and was quite surprised when Iris nodded. So we continued our intense conversation in my room.

No, we didn't end up in bed. We waited until our wedding night, six months later. After all, my wife is a person of principles.

By the way, we still distribute the *War Cry* together. And not only in the run-down station district, but everywhere. We have no borders now.

The Loving Husband

The other day I woke up with a hangover, at least it felt that way, even though the night before I had only had a glass of red wine. Somehow I felt limp all day long, the hours stretched out like a long rubber band.

A slight headache in the evening made me even more irritable, and in order not to annoy my hard-working husband and not to spoil his well-deserved hours of rest, I decided to go to bed early.

"Good night, darling!" "Sleep well, darling!"

I kissed him on both cheeks and left him sitting alone in front of the TV with a bottle of beer.

My husband is the dream image of a spouse, and you can't praise him enough in the family circle and before visits. He is intelligent, has the pleasing appearance of a sportsman and the necessary amount of hair on his chest to attract the attention of curious women on the street. He likes to help around the house. Shopping and washing up are his hobbies. He does not smoke, is not a drinker, and although he is middle-aged, he still does not have a beer belly. The latter is my secret pride, because this is rare among men, especially in our community.

Victoria, my dear friend in the old homeland of Italy, and more than often visiting our industrial stand this side of the big pond has for long envied my domestic happiness and has often tried to discover a hidden vice in my husband. To this day, however, she has been unsuccessful in her efforts.

"You have a real treasure at home, my dear," everyone tells me, and I completely agree with them. So on this evening, I left my loved husband in peace and dedicated myself to the preservation of my own well-being. After fifteen years of marriage, I knew with certainty that no shocking deeds were to be feared from him. He would drink his good beer, have some homemade hot dogs, watch foodie videos on the Internet, and go to bed—all quite normal. And since I'm no friend of swallowing pills, I made myself a fragrant St. Johns tea, which is said to calm your nerves, and brought it to bed.

A light read would additionally help to gradually transport me into the realm of dreams. This familiar recipe had always worked until now. Only this evening, it did not. I read one story after the other, drank five cups of the calming tea and became increasingly awake.

A tiny little man with thin legs wriggled in my brain, scratching and tugging around never allowing me to sleep. Shortly before midnight, the restlessness had increased to such an extent that I couldn't stand it in bed anymore. I decided to slip into my flip-flops, put on the T-shirt that reached down to my knees and carefully opened the door to the living room.

Well, if the tea doesn't help, I'll just try a glass of wine in the company of my treasure, I thought.

As expected, the treasure sat in his armchair with his back to me staring at his laptop.

"Darling, I absolutely can't fall asleep," I groaned and wanted to ask for permission to sit with him.

He looked up in shock, and his face turned red. He hurriedly closed his laptop and threw it on the couch. The beer bottle fell over and a small irregular dark spot formed on the light-colored carpet.

"But what is it," I stuttered in surprise, "am I disturbing you?"

The laptop slowly slid off the couch and landed on the carpet. I could clearly see a catalog of an erotic shop with samples, my husband had been studying it. Next to it were two large empty paper cups of Ben and Jerry's ice cream. I became quite confused, felt my face turn pale, and a slight tingling in my fingers announced impending fainting.

My athletic, efficient and generally exemplary husband, his mother-in-law's favorite and a joy for the eyes of many women ate ice cream in large quantities and enjoyed eroticism!

In my mind's eye appeared a heavy, diabetic male being with flabby round cheeks, bad teeth and foul breath. His belly spilled out from his trousers, and the last two buttons were missing from his shirt. The human smacked with chocolate-glued lips reached to caress me. A nightmare!

Suddenly I had to yawn loud and wide. The shock had an unexpected effect on me, and I became uncontrollably sleepy. Tiredness finally took over with a force that I was unable to resist. With weak knees, I turned around, left my husband with the consequences of his weak character and plodded back to the bedroom to follow the needs of nature. Just before I dozed off, I prayed for a few seconds.

The next day, a Sunday, my husband seemed very serious.

"So, what are we going to do today," he asked.

For a few seconds, I just stared at him thoughtfully.

"You didn't criticize me one bit yesterday. I need a change." He shrugged. "Do you want to go to church? We have a nice one in town, we've never been to before."

The Evil Double Life

He didn't know whether it was the strangest situation in his life, or something new, a kind of unknown power that had met him for the first time. He was about to draw a pistol when a ray of light appeared, and a bright translucent arm stretched out towards him with an open hand. Someone wanted to help him — darkness and light. And then the monotonous, shrill sound of the alarm clock ripping him from his sleep. What a strange dream. It was now five-thirty in the morning. Still sleepy, he groped with his left hand for the device to turn off the ringing.

Slowly he pulled himself together. What a shitty day today. He rubbed his eyes, yawned, and ran his fingers through his short, tousled hair.

His pajamas were wrinkled, and Oliver was a little annoyed to have been torn so brutally from his beautiful dream. He had already forgotten what he had dreamed about, but he had no doubt that it had been beautiful. When he fell back on his pillow, he noticed saliva dribbling from his mouth, whereupon he threw the pillow to the foot of the bed in disgust.

"Honey, what time is it? Do you always have to leave so early?" groaned a drowsy voice coming from the indefinable pile of long, dark hair and blanket lying next to him.

"You know how that works," he said, trying to sound reasonably cheerful. Always think positively, Elisabeth used to say, and that's exactly what he was going to do this morning. It would probably be hard, but you didn't have to let it show right away.

Oliver got out of bed quietly, slipped into his slippers and headed for the bathroom, careful to be as silent as possible so his wife could continue sleeping.

The water was cold. Pretty cold, but it was just what he needed. "Start the day in a good mood, then you'll do your job even better," he murmured to himself.

After he had shaved and applied deodorant, and aftershave, he also felt much fresher. While brushing his teeth, he crept into the bedroom as quietly as possible and put on his silver Rolex, which he had placed on the bedside table the night before. When he had finished, he went to the training and dressing room.

The room was about twenty square meters and was dominated by an elongated, externally mirrored cabinet, which was juxtaposed with various exercise machines — an exercise bike, a treadmill and various weight-lifting options.

Oliver worked out regularly in the evenings, so all he needed in the mornings, were fifty push-ups and an equal number of sit-ups to get his circulation going without breaking out in a sweat.

Oliver drank his morning coffee black and without sugar, but in return, he enjoyed plenty of orange juice and vitamin-enriched energy drinks as a counterbalance. While he had toast, first with peanut butter and then with orange marmalade, he casually scrolled through his cell phone—nothing important apparently, which confirmed his thoughts. In fact, he wasn't really interested in it, but he made sure to answer all messages briefly. The Eagles boomed from the speakers of his three-thousand-dollar Bose stereo system.

Oliver preferred Armani. He put on the crisp white shirt, slipped into his elegant, tailor-made anthracite suit and tied the tie knot. He then grabbed the business bag, which he had already packed the night before, and prepared to leave his house discreetly—a last look in the mirror. Perfect.

6:20. The metro was, of course, delayed, as it was every day. But Oliver had already taken that into account. As usual, it wasn't very full, but it would fill up along the thirty-minute ride, and by the time he finally got off, it would become quite cramped. He reached his destination, the central station, not a moment too early. Oliver, like most people, didn't really feel comfortable in large crowds, but he didn't have too much of a problem with that either. The more people stayed in one place, the less he attracted attention in the crowd. He liked that.

Oliver wore a black trench coat, so he was spared unpleasant questions about his clothes and appearance.

It was now 6:45 am, and he got out to get back into another carriage. The fat black woman opposite him had been staring for too long. He decided never to ride in the first carriage again. Oliver wondered if he should try something now and then, do something stupid. It would be fun to count to three and punch the old auntie in the brain.

Oliver's head shake was barely noticeable. *Not today*, he thought. But, he hoped there weren't any more deviant creatures like that old bag or even migrants. Still, the old aunt had had such a strange look, who was she? The important thing was that she finally looked away.

Exactly twenty minutes later he got off at the central station. Then he only had to walk two blocks further to reach his destination. Wharton Business Building.

Oliver greeted the doorman with a subtle nod, and marched purposefully toward the elevator, picking up his pace just before he entered the company's open-glass door.

"Hey, Porter, how are you doing this morning?"

Oliver turned. Right behind the door was O'Neill, the old bastard. Oliver nodded at the fat middle-aged man and tried something similar, a polite smile.

O'Neill was an unpleasant colleague whom he usually ignored.

"Still on Junior's Account?" asked O'Neill, whose weather-beaten skin looked as if it would completely rot off in ten years at the latest. Oliver had to control himself not to make a disgusted face.

"Oh... of course," he replied and put on a playful grin that was meant to express satisfaction and a little bragging. Feelings that he actually didn't have. He just didn't care about it at the moment.

"Wow, then you must really be the lucky one," said O'Neill with a laugh and patted Oliver on the shoulder.

It was supposed to represent something like cordiality, Oliver thought and chewed at his jaw, although he had nothing in his mouth.

In the long hallway, the two men were met by a young, attractive woman in a cream-colored trouser suit, probably Yves Saint Lauren. Maybe twenty-eight. *Definitely a fucking fuckable* thing, Oliver mused. He caught himself looking at her and noticed, slightly amused, O'Neill staring at her bottom. *Old, ugly fuck, forget it. Just forget it. If anything, that's mine, one way or another.*

They reached the company's reception hall. Luckily, O'Neill would turn left here. That saved him at least some of the stupid, petty chatter that would undoubtedly still await him.

But no, this couldn't be true, today fat O'Neill followed him.

"I heard Cherry and Todd got caught doing something," offered O'Neill.

The chatter was now almost pre-programmed. The man was just rewinding a voice recorder that some crazy surgeon had transplanted behind his vocal cords.

"Did you know they were involved? I'm not a big fan of this woman's talk," he chuckled, "but it's worth a few words about it."

In another ten yards or five seconds, he would reach his office.

"That's it," Oliver said. "It was nice talking to you... uh... O'Neill, right?"

O'Neill winked at him and snapped his finger in a playful gesture. *What a jerk.*

No sooner had Oliver taken a seat behind his screen when he saw a dark figure coming towards him from the corner of his eye.

"Ah, Mr Porter. Good to see you," a sonorous female voice called out to him. It was Elli Marples. She worked in an office two corridors away and was a Jones, Meyer and Champs employee, a second-rate law firm in Oliver's opinion, but with a first-class reputation — at least if you believed Elli. Since he had begun working here, the old smoker, who was in her late forties, always greeted him in an over-friendly way.

"You're looking sharp, Olli. May I call you Olli?" She dropped her eyes with a hint of embarrassment. "In the meantime, we can get to know each other a little."

"Of course," Oliver replied with a suppressed smile.

But he knew immediately that this worn-out frigate was flirting with him for business reasons only. Oliver had long since given up having any illusions about people, especially women, although he trusted his wife, so far.

The day went by meaninglessly, phone calls, letters, accountant crap. But he stayed focused, nothing upset him, he was quite proud about that. And still, one day less.

Oliver was on his way home, not far from the metro. He walked nervously through a pedestrian tunnel and finally arrived at the somewhat run-down apartment building where he had rented a small apartment. Nobody seemed to be there except the caretaker, who was probably repairing something somewhere in the basement.

"Hey mister," shouted a voice, greeting him, when Oliver was on the stairs between the second and the third floor. The caretaker had an oriental accent. He was probably an Indian or a Pakistani.

"Good evening," Oliver returned dryly.

"Please do not enter the basement. There has been a small mishap down here. Please excuse me."

"No problem." Oliver now looked down the hallway through the railing so he could see the man below. He smiled affirmatively.

He continued up the hallway until he finally arrived at a door. It was quite a simple door, but sturdy and soundproof. Oliver had installed it himself. An exact replica of the original. There was a peephole at eye level through which people standing in the corridor could be observed. He unlocked the door and entered the small apartment. Opposite the entrance was a window darkened by a roller shutter. In front of it was a desk with a laptop sitting on it. Oliver turned the computer on.

The room was sparsely furnished. The table. A revolving chair. Two high, angular cupboards. Oliver opened one of them and grabbed a revolver from the top shelf. Sitting in his chair, he playfully spun the drum.

He opened the drawer under the tabletop. Inside were several disposable cell phones — without a contract. He turned one on and checked a few of the numbers stored in it. At the same time, he typed something into the computer. Shortly afterwards he closed the program, and for a fraction of a second, the desktop showed the picture of a young, well-dressed gentleman.

Oliver put on a headset and turned on another program. *Let's see if one of my middlemen has a new assignment for me.*

While he was waiting for the software to load, he dug out a packet of bullets and played with them, slipping them one by one between his fingers. He glanced into the next room. The door was open. Only the reddish glow of small high-tech devices could be seen — otherwise, the room was dark. It was precisely three minutes past eight.

At that exact same time, Elisabeth was sitting on her white couch with a glass of red wine. She was scanning through a magazine on the wide-screen plasma TV on the topic, *Sleep Disorders — A sign of a disturbed relationship with the employer?* And was about to fall asleep.

Of course, she could not relate to the subject matter of the program. At least not really. She had never worked before. She had married Oliver right after university. She had actually grown up in a strict Catholic home although she didn't believe in conservative, bourgeois role relationships. Then again, it was her husband who brought the money home. He earned really well, but he worked such terribly long hours, at least that's what she thought.

Quite often, Oliver would come home very late. And this was one of those days. She waited impatiently, wanting nothing more than to be taken in his arms. It had been such a disaster for her... She sighed and closed her eyes briefly.

Suddenly a small red dot appeared in the darkness from her bedroom window. After a few seconds, the dot multiplied to many dots, which slowly came closer. Had she paid closer attention, she would certainly have heard a soft rustling from outside, but Elisabeth was completely lost in thought. Her glass was empty, and she stood up, striding towards the kitchen, to pour herself another one.

Finally, she heard the familiar turning of the key in the door. Olli. At last. She smelled his perfume, yes, it was him. The hallway light came on. She saw his shadow on the floor.

"Honey? Where were you? I had a terribly long day," she said, moaning exaggeratedly.

Silence. A moment passed.

"Honey?"

A short moment of silence, then she stuck her head out of the half-opened door.

It was her husband. He was pale.

"Olli, What happened?"

"Nothing. I believe nothing. I was just thinking...I might have heard something."

"My love," Elisabeth said. Ignoring Oliver's words of concern.

At that very moment, a loud clicking sound was heard. Glass shattered and with a loud bang, the door opened behind them. Many men in black erupted into the house.

Oliver didn't know what to do. He reached into the inside pocket of his long, dark coat and pulled out something silvery. But before he could react, there was a soft click and a bullet drilled into his head. He collapsed lifelessly to the floor. A second of silence followed the thud of his fall. Then Elisabeth started to scream. She screamed as loud and as long as she could. Strange looking silhouettes appeared just before she dropped to her knees out of shock and despair. She recognized the letters SWAT printed in white on the dark creatures that had stormed into the room.

Later on, just before midnight, Elizabeth was huddled up on a couch somewhere, wrapped in a warm blanket. Next to her sat a police psychologist and a doctor who had given her a Valium. She had suffered a terrible shock.

The silver object that Oliver had tried to pull out of his coat had been a cell phone, not a gun. She realized they had shot the wrong man, her husband.

The only gun he had was a 38 caliber revolver legally registered in his name. They must have broken into the wrong house. The mistake was unforgivable, and the officer in charge would probably be suspended for the time being. Next door to the Porters lived a man named Sammy Smith. A professional killer, who under the name 'tin man' had been carrying out assassinations for the Mafia and their employers for years.

However, in Oliver's coat pocket, a memory stitch with a video in it was recovered. As it turned out, he earned most of his income by shooting and distributing gay porn with a tragic-comic plot. Not as a successful accountant, as his wife had always believed.

The frame on the videotape which the district attorney Schmidt used to narrate the fatal events and strange double life to his colleagues, revealed naked men on a large bed in a cramped room. In the background, a half-open door was visible. It led to another sparsely furnished room where one could just make out a few angular cupboards, a table on which a laptop was placed, in front of a rotating chair.

Only years later, Elisabeth found out that her husband had been trying to change his job, possibly his life, years before the accident. From old documents, letters and emails, she could tell that he had visited a priest only one day before his death. When she found out, Elizabeth got down on her knees and cried.

If he had tried earlier, everything would have been different, flashed through her mind.

This was all a year ago. Now, Elizabeth led a quasi-new life, had even found a new partner, and her job satisfied her more. It was the darkness of that time that helped her find new ways. She remembered her depression had become so strong that she had had a spiritual experience. Since then, her life had become better, although only very slowly. Not perfect, but with spiritual progression.

The Dying Veteran

Two men, both veterans and seriously ill, were lying in a standard hospital room of a clinic. One was allowed to sit up in his bed for an hour each day to drain the fluid from his lungs. His bed was right by the window. The other man had to lie flat on his back all day.

The men chatted for hours on end. They talked about their wives, their families, their professions, what they had done during their military service and where they went on holiday.

Every afternoon, when the man was allowed to sit up in the bed by the window, he spent his time describing to his roommate all the things he could see outside the window.

The man in the other bed started to live for those one-hour intervals when his world would expand and be enlivened by the events and colors of the outside world!

The window overlooked a park with a charming lake. Ducks and swans glided over the water, as he watched runners jogging their rounds and young lovers strolling arm in arm among the multi-colored flowers. The magnificent silhouette of the city was visible in the distance. When the man at the window described all these things in incredible detail, the man on the other side of the room closed his eyes and imagined the picturesque scene.

On a warm holiday afternoon, the man at the window described a high school musical parade that was just passing by. Although the other man couldn't hear the parade, he could see it clearly — with his mind's eye, because the man at the window described it with such impressive words.

Days and weeks went by. One morning, just as the nurse was coming to wash the two men, she found the man at the window lifeless — he had died peacefully in his sleep. She was sad and called the hospital assistant to take the dead man away.

As soon as it seemed appropriate, the other man asked if he could now switch to the bed by the window. The nurse gladly allowed this, and as soon as he seemed comfortable, she left him alone. Slowly and painfully, he leaned on his elbow with difficulty to get a first glimpse of the world outside. He strained himself and turned to the side to look out the window next to the bed. Opposite the window stood a naked wall. The man called the nurse and asked her what could have moved his roommate to describe such wonderful things outside the window?

The sister replied, "Maybe he was trying to cheer you up. Did you know that the man was blind and couldn't even see the wall outside the window? But maybe that's why he saw more than we did."

The Old Bridge

The bridge in the village stretched high and far across the small river that divided the houses and their inhabitants into two groups. Throughout the year the river that flowed under the bridge was only a small trickle, but once the snow had melted in spring or after long rainy days in autumn it swelled, and the bridge was then the only way to visit the other side.

But the bridge was more than just a connection between the two banks. It offered a magnificent view of the valley and room for a little entertainment; it was a meeting place for lovers and a sales area for traveling salesmen. And — it was a sign.

Legend has it that, long before the houses became a village, there were two farms to the left and right of the river, which offered their inhabitants little income. The work was hard, and the land barren. There was little money left to buy new and practical tools that made the work easier and offered the opportunity for some prosperity. Again and again, both farmers thought about building a bridge. But if there was hardly enough money for a new plow or for more cattle, even less for a bridge.

Until one year, a terrible drought hit the country. The harvest was even scarcer, the seeds barely sprouted and the cattle had little meat on their bones and hardly gave any milk.

The river dried up completely. And so it happened that the families were able to get to the other side without difficulty — and they helped each other as they could. When the farmer on the left side could no longer sow the seeds, the farmer on the right side would come to his aid. And when the cow on the right side was about to calve, the farmer on the other side offered good advice, and they took turns to guard the stable. Despite the drought, both families were better off at the end of the year than ever before.

The next year the rain came again. This time both families started to build the bridge over the river, even if there was hardly any money and even less time. But experience had taught them that sometimes it was best to invest the little you had in a bridge that would allow them to unite.

The bridge would allow the people to connect in all seasons, as well as in good and bad times.

Ever since then the families have prospered because of their closeness, whether the river runs dry or floods.

The True Story of Friar Max Kolbe

A prisoner has escaped from the concentration camp.

In the evening, camp leader Fritsch steps before the prisoners.

"The fugitive has not been found," he yells. "Ten of you will die for this in the hunger bunker."

He approaches the first row and looks everyone sharply in the eye. Suddenly he raises his hand, points his finger.

"Him!"

Pale as a sheet, the man steps out of line.

"You, and you — and you too."

The condemned step forward, unable to react, like sheep being led to the slaughterhouse.

"Now you're 10. 10 men sentenced to death."

One of them takes his cap off and begs, "Oh, please spare me, I have a poor wife and children!"

Fritsch stares at the creature in contempt.

Suddenly something unexpected happens. Another prisoner steps out of line and stops in front of Fritsch. The camp leader reaches for his revolver.

"Stop! What does this Polish pig want from me?"

The prisoner calmly replies, "I want to die instead of this condemned man!"

"Who are you?"

"A Catholic priest."

A moment of silence follows. Finally, Fritsch makes his decision and says in a hoarse voice, "Agreed! Go with them! Death by starvation for you as well."

Thus the Franciscan Maximilian Kolbe died at the age of forty-seven. A man who wanted to conquer the world through love. But he knew that, *no one shows greater love than he who gives his life for his friends.*

The Emperor's Gifts

Koxinga, the Emperor of Japan, had recovered from a serious illness against all hopes. So he called his advisers and said, "Today I would like to know what you think of me. Do you believe that I am a good emperor? Speak the truth without fear. As a token for your open and honest opinion, I would like to give each of you a jewel."

One after the other, the advisers came forward with fine words and exaggerated praise.

When it was the turn of the wisest of the advisers, he said, "My Emperor, I would rather keep silent, for the truth cannot be bought."

The emperor said, "Very well. Then you will receive nothing. So, now you can speak your mind."

Then the respected aide-de-camp Yoshima said, "My Emperor, you want to know what I think. I think that you are a person with many weaknesses who makes mistakes, just like us. But your mistakes are much more serious. All the people groan under the burden of taxes, and as a commander, you are a failure. I think you spend too much money celebrating festivals and building new palaces."

When the emperor heard this, he became thoughtful. Then he handed out one gem to each of his advisers, as he had promised. But he appointed Yoshima as his chancellor.

The next day the flatterers appeared before the emperor.

"My Emperor," said the spokesman, "the merchant who sold you these jewels should be hanged! For the stones you gave us are false."

"I have known that for a long time," the emperor replied. "they are as false as your words."

Puppies for Sale

A shop owner had nailed a sign over his door that read 'Puppies for sale'. The sign attracted children. Soon a little boy appeared and asked, "How much do they sell the babies for?"

The owner said, "Between 30 and 50 dollars."

The little boy reached into his pocket and pulled out some change. "I have two and a quarter, can I have a look at them?"

The owner grinned and whistled. Out of the kennel came a dog named Lady, she ran down the aisle of his shop, followed by five puppies. One of them was walking alone, visibly far behind the others. Immediately the boy saw the limping little one and asked, "What's wrong with this little dog?"

The man explained that when the little one was born, the vet said it had broken a joint and would limp for the rest of its life.

The little boy yelled out excitingly, "Let me have him. I want to buy that little dog!"

The man replied, "No, you don't want to buy the little dog. If you really want the puppy, I'll give it to you."

The little boy was confused. He looked straight into the man's eyes and said, "I don't want the puppy as a gift. It's worth as much as the other dogs, and I want to pay full price. I'll give you what I've got now, and pay you 10 dollars every month until I pay off my debt."

The man shook his head. "You really don't have to pay for this dog, son. It'll never be able to run, bounce or play like the other little dogs."

The boy reached down and rolled up the leg of his pants, and showed his badly bent, crippled left leg, splinted with a thick metal bar.

He looked up at the man and said, "Listen, I can't run very well either, and the little dog needs someone who'll understand it."

The man bit his lower lip. Tears came to his eyes, he smiled and said, "My son, I hope and pray that each one of these little puppies will have an owner like you."

The Future Kingdom of Peace

It was the time before electricity and a time in which faith sometimes came out stronger and in some places often became weaker again. It was not a time of wealth, especially in the villages.

In this last village before the mountains and the hinterland, the snow fell softly and enveloped the landscape in a white cloth. The hands of the church clock tower had just passed the midnight hour. Almost everything was dark. The only visible light came from one small window. In a room behind the window, an old man lay in his bed. A few people stood around the bed and talked in whispers. You could see that the old man was coming to the end of his days. An elderly woman sat on a chair next to the bed and struggled with tears while she lovingly stroked the old man's head.

A flickering candle stood on a table and gave the darkened room a somewhat mystical shimmer with its dancing light.

Again and again, you could see a slight twitch in the old man's features, as if wanting to express a happy smile.

As in a film, scenes from past days flashed by his inner eye, he suddenly muttered something, and everyone in the room interrupted their quiet conversations and tried to read his lips or catch a word. Then it was quiet again for a short time.

He had experienced so much in his lifetime! Once he had traveled the world as a traveling salesman. He knew the Great Wall of China, and the pyramids of Egypt were not unknown to him. His travels took him to the most distant corners of the world. He had always had an eye for the people around him. What misery and need he had witnessed!

Some people were oppressors. The one with the most power exploited the other.

If there were small uprisings or even great revolutions somewhere and circumstances changed, sooner or later the previously enslaved person ended up being as much as an oppressor as the one who had been usurped.

Often the fear of losing newly acquired wealth or power made them act worse than their predecessors. If they still shouted a lot about equality and brotherhood or other 'high aims', it seemed in the end not to concern them, but always the others. Some shouted old phrases like 'Turn the swords into plowshares', but if a few did so, the others, who still had their weapons, often took advantage of the situation shamelessly to seize power.

When will there finally be peace? The man asked himself many a time. *Would there ever be such a world where all people could live together in harmony and peace?* He was not sure, for he saw again and again that evil was within man, and it was only a question of time before circumstances brought this to light. If somebody had wealth, they all craved for a share and presented themselves as good friends. And when the wealth had vanished, the so praised friendship was mostly over. How could peace ever reign in such a world where everyone thought only of themselves and their well-being?

The church tower bells rang to signal the next full hour. It was now two o'clock in the morning. In the evening the bells would sound longer than usual because it was Christmas Eve and people would traditionally fill the churches. I wondered if the old man would live to see this evening when the birth of the Son of God is celebrated.

With half an ear, the man heard the bells ringing. His thoughts went back several years to a special Christmas Eve.

It had been a bitterly, cold and stormy day. Actually, the man had not much to do with faith in God. But on this evening he too had attended the Christmas service because his daughter and grandchildren had invited him to do so.

"Well, there's no harm in taking a look at the nativity scene," he muttered to himself and followed his loved ones. But when heard in the sermon, he could hardly believe his ears. Suddenly it was as if God Himself had opened his eyes and ears when there was mention of what the angels sang at Jesus's birth. What had the angels sung at that time?

"Glory to God in the highest and peace on earth among men of his good pleasure," was read from the Bible.

Had he, a man who was quite respectable, also deserved God's pleasure? Until now, he had not cared about God and His will. How then could he have pleased God?

Then it was further quoted from the Bible, "For unto us a child is born, and a son is given unto us, and the kingdom shall be upon his shoulder; and his name is called Wonderful Counselor, God—Hero, Eternal Father, Prince of Peace."

"Prince of Peace," he repeated thoughtfully under his breath. Wasn't that what he always missed so much in the world? A ruler of Peace who would bring peace to the people? But had Jesus at that time brought peace to the world? He knew only too well that Jesus was rejected by most people, who had thus chosen to refuse peace. Until today, nothing had changed. But had not Jesus set an example? Yes, Jesus Himself lived exactly the way he had taught others to! He embodied in his appearance those values on which a new, just and peaceful world can grow. And in doing so, he had left the glory as Creator and King of all kings and had come to earth as a simple, humble man. Even his birth had taken place in a stable. No revolutionary would have humiliated himself like that. Later, when this Jesus had disciples who followed him, he even washed their feet! The man was sure that there had never been anything like it in history.

He remembered what he had once heard, that Jesus would one day build a new kingdom of peace. At that thought, the man had to sigh a little. Yes, he would like to be there!

Suddenly he was ripped from his thoughts. One of his grandchildren was pulling at his sleeve and shouting, "Grandpa, the service is over! Come on home!"

"Yes, I'm coming," slipped from his lips, but with his mind, he was still thinking about what had been said. He wanted to be with that Prince of Peace, that was now his firm decision.

As the sinner in the temple in Jesus's parable, he beat his chest, inwardly, "Lord, be merciful to me, the sinner." With this cry of the heart, he followed the grandchildren outside. A wonderful peace had settled in his heart.

When he went to bed and fell asleep, he had a dream that impressed him very much.

In this dream, he stood on a high mountain and saw the sinful world down in the valley, much uglier and more repulsive than ever before. Hatred, jealousy, greed, resentment, lies and deceit and much more, wherever he looked.

Suddenly, heavenly trumpets sounded. The sky was torn in two and glorious light flooded around him. Angels came to meet him, took him by the hand and led him up to this light.

What he saw there can hardly be described. Such splendor and glory were almost unbearable to an untrained eye. Everything was flooded with bright, warm, loving and peaceful light. Everything was pure and crystal clear. The streets were of gold and the gates studded with pure and glorious gems. He knew a lot about gemstones, for he had traded in jewelry, gold and precious stones all over the world. But what he saw here was out of proportion to what he used to call beautiful.

But that was not all. People there met each other with respect. Each seemed intent on preceding the other in reverence. One respected the other more than he respected himself. There was a wonderful harmony. Then he saw a throne in the centre of the city, from which light and peace radiated to every corner. Everything seemed to emanate from the throne of God. Nowhere could he see suffering or even tears.

Suddenly he realized why the Bible spoke so emphatically that no unclean person and no one who loved sin was allowed to move in here. Only the one who had the disposition of the one who sat on the throne and loved his fellow-men could move in here, for otherwise this harmony would be disturbed.

Now he understood the meaning of the highest commandment, 'You shall love the Lord your God with all your heart, with all your soul, with all your strength and with all your mind, and your neighbor as yourself.'

It was the most wonderful dream he had ever had.

The clock struck again. The chime hadn't faded away for long when a deep but peaceful sigh made all those standing around the bed gather around.

The old man's face was radiant — a radiance of bright joy. Then everything became very quiet, only the soft ticking of the clock on the bedside table could be heard. Had he been allowed to see some of the glory before he went over there?

The Horseman

As a former cavalryman in the once great army, the man had remained proud all these decades, proud that he was still able to ride and be respected as a horseman. And this ride was his last, his final return home to his homeland, but he was still far from where the adventure of his life began decades ago.

The man rode his horse along a dirt road. He was not aware of how long he had been on the road. Maybe hours or decades. He was enjoying the view, and suddenly he realized that he had died. He remembered his death and that his horse had died many years before, and he wondered where the road would take him.

After a while, he came to a high white wall that ran along the road. It looked like fine marble. Far off, on the top of the hill, in the sunlight, a large archway gleamed. As he got closer, he saw that the magnificent archway looked like a far castle, almost like a dream castle out of this world, and the road leading to the archway looked like pure gold.

But even as he tried to get closer, the distance seemed to remain the same. He and his horse rode towards the seemingly endless marble wall until they reached what looked like a gate. Just as they were about to enter, they saw a man in a dark robe and hood, sitting on a boulder on the side.

When he got close enough, the rider asked, "Excuse me, where are we?"

"This is Heaven, my son," the man replied.

"Is that right? Would it be possible to get some water?" asked the rider.

"Of course, sir, just come in, and I'll bring you a glass of water with ice right away."

The man on the boulder made a gesture, and the gate began to open.

The rider pointed to his horse and asked, "May my friend come in as well?"

But the man bowed his head. "I'm very sorry, but animals are not allowed in here."

The rider pondered for a moment and then he turned back to the road and rode away. After a long ride and up another steep hill, he came to a dirt path leading to a farm that looked as if it had never been gated before. There was no clear entrance either, and as he gradually reached the farmhouse, he saw a man leaning against a tree reading a book.

"Excuse me!" he shouted to the reader, "Do you have any water?"

"Sure, there's a pump behind the tree."

The reader pointed to a barely visible gate. "Go through that gate, and come in."

"What about my friend here?" asked the rider, pointing to his horse.

"There should be a bucket by the pump."

They walked through the gate, and behind some bushes, there was an old-fashioned hand pump with a bucket beside it. The rider filled the bucket with water, took a big gulp and then he gave the horse some. When they had quenched their thirst, they went over to the man who was waiting for them by the tree.

"What do you call this place?" asked the horseman.

"This here is Heaven," was the answer.

"This is very confusing," said the horseman. "Because down the road across the hill, there was a strange fellow who also said the place was Heaven."

"Oh, you mean that place with the marble wall and the golden road that leads to a castle? No, that's hell."

"But he said it was Heaven. Doesn't it annoy you that they take your name unjustly?"

"No, but I can understand you are confused, but we're actually quite happy that he calls his place Heaven as well because the truth is revealed by their actions."

"Meaning what?"

"Did he not refuse your horse, which is part of your spirit and existence?"

"We are basically the same."

"See, and he refused you. And those who have been refused are ending up here in the real heaven because that's how they filter out the people who abandon their best friends."

The Major

"I was a major in the military. Then I came under the power of alcohol and could not be freed. My wife tormented herself with me for a long time until she finally took our two children and moved in with her parents. She left the apartment to me, but I needed money and eventually lost the apartment. Little by little, I sold everything, my car, my gun, even my clothes.

I found shelter in a dilapidated house.

"This is no life," an angry voice whispered to me, "why torture yourself more? Take a rope and hang yourself!"

With such thoughts, I was walking through the streets of Detroit when a woman came up to me and said, "Oh, you poor unfortunate man, you look like you need help. May I ask why you've become homeless?"

I said I was a veteran, but alcohol, illness and circumstances had put me on the street.

"Do you have any idea how to get back on your feet?"

I told her about my half-baked ideas, as far as they made sense at all.

"Here is a gospel. In it, there is a tract. Read it, you will find good things in there. When you've finished, come and see me at the church office."

She gave me her business card. A congregation with an address in a high-rise building downtown that I'd never heard of, but it didn't matter.

I went back to my safe house, and I started reading the tract. It made it easier on my heart. Then I read the Gospel and learned that all people are sinners and that Jesus died for sinners. This made me think and gave me strength for indefinable reasons.

I still can't explain the details exactly to this day, but after reading the Gospel, I was not the same anymore. In a short time, I became a member of this, I must say, almost secret church, on the top floor of the building that officially was not allowed to exist. There I converted and filled my heart with joy. Then I began to look for believers.

The most unbelievable things happened in a short time. Other believers became my friends. An unknown person in our church, where only the pure Gospel was its center, gave me a job as an elevator installer. As a vet, I was supposed to be suitable for the job.

In my spare time, I actively searched for people who were still suffering, such as alcoholics, addicts, depressed, people who seemed to have forgotten society. All I did was talk to them casually and asked if they needed to talk, offering them our community's business card.

I still don't know how I got there, but one day, I was standing outside my ex's door. She was shocked to see me and said she hardly recognized me. She told me my figure and face had changed. After a short conversation, she said she could hardly believe it was me, and that she wanted an explanation. A few weeks later, I was reunited with my family.

A Strange Dream

Since I got off the pills, I sleep deeper. Of course, I had been taking the tablets for years, but it was no longer possible, I had to get off them. Nothing else happened, but my life became better, especially physically. My sleep was no longer like a coma and was again filled with dreams, but more real, more fantastic, sometimes strange, but I usually couldn't remember them.

Then the other day, I had another dream. In this dream, I found myself in a strange room. There were no special features there, except a wall littered with small old-fashioned index card boxes, similar to those found in libraries in the past. But these card boxes, of which there seemed to be an endless number, had extraordinary titles.

When I approached the card index boxes, the first one that caught my eye had the words, 'Girl I once liked' written on it. I pulled out the drawer and started leafing through the records. At that moment, I pushed the drawer back again. I was shocked because I immediately recognized the names written there. And then, without having been told, I suddenly knew exactly where I was.

This lifeless room with all its small index cards was an unembellished cataloging system of my life. All the deeds and thoughts of my life were recorded here in such detail that my memory could not come close to keeping up with them.

A feeling of amazement and curiosity, mixed with horror, pervaded me as I began to randomly open different boxes and examine their contents. Some of them brought me joy and pleasant memories. Others I felt ashamed of, for they brought a feeling of remorse, so intense that I looked over my shoulder to see if I was being observed.

There was a file called 'Friends' next to a file called 'Friends I betrayed'. There were all kinds of different files. Some were absolutely ordinary, such as, 'Books I read', Jokes I laughed at'. Some were rather strange like, 'School hours I slept in', 'Favorite objects of my mother I broke', 'Work I shirked'. Some were really funny in terms of their accuracy, 'Nasty things I threw at my brother's head', others I couldn't laugh at all. 'Things I did in anger', 'Quarrels I started'.

I was always surprised by the contents of the index card boxes. Often there were many more index cards than I expected, then again, sometimes less than I had hoped to find. Nevertheless, I was amazed by the amount of information about the life I've lived. Could it be possible that in all the years I had created each of these thousands, even millions of cards myself? So far, every card confirmed that assumption. They were all written in my handwriting — they all bore my signature.

When I pulled out the index card, 'Songs I have heard', I saw no end to it. The cards were tightly packed, and seemed endless. Ashamed, I closed the box again, not because of the quality of the music, but rather because of the vast amount of time I had wasted, as it was so clear by now.

When I came to a file entitled 'Lustful thoughts', I felt a shiver running through my limbs. I pulled the box out an inch or two, not wanting its full length revealed to me. I pulled out a card. I shivered when I noticed its detailed contents.

I felt sick at the thought that such a moment had been recorded. I felt anger and panic rising within me. A single thought dominated in my head, *Never let anyone see these cards! No one must ever see this room! I absolutely must destroy all this.*

In an almost insane rage, I tore the box out of the wall. Its size was no longer important. I had to empty it and burn the cards. I took the box in one swing and smashed it on the floor, but then, like in a nightmare nothing, no cards came loose. Desperately I tried to rip out a single card with both hands, but my endeavor was futile, for it was anchored and unbreakable. Weary and totally helpless, I shoved it back into the box.

With my arms down by my sides and my head resting against the wall, I stood there and sighed out loud with pity. All of this could not be true. And then I saw it. The title was, 'People to whom I have brought the Gospel'.

This box looked better than the others, newer, almost unused. I wanted to pull it out, but there wasn't much to pull out of it. I could count the cards with the finger of one hand. My eyes filled with tears. Somehow I started to cry, with a sob so deep that it hurt my stomach and shook me completely. I cried out in pain from the overwhelming shame I felt. The index card boxes blurred before my tear-filled eyes.

No one — no one must ever know about this room. I must lock it up and hide the key where no one can find it. But then for a split second, it occurred to me. What if this all was just a dream, what if I could still make amends? What if I could continue to bring the Gospel out? The outcome would be different, for sure, probably the indexes would be arranged differently, most likely the whole room would be different. And with the grasp of this thought, I didn't want this alternative outcome to be a dream. I wanted to become this reality.

The Boulder

One night a man was awakened from his sleep by the Lord, who showed him a huge rock lying in front of his log cabin.

The Lord said, "Press against this rock with all your might."

That's what the man did for years, for hours every day he toiled in sunshine, rain and snow. Every evening he was utterly exhausted, thinking that he had worked in vain because the rock never moved.

He said, "Lord, I have worked long and hard in your ministry and put all my strength into what you have asked me to do. But I have not been able to move that boulder an inch. What's the matter? Why am I such a failure?"

The Lord replied, "My son, I asked you to serve me and to press against this rock with all your might, and you were obedient. I did not ask you to push it away. I only asked you to brace yourself against it. And now you think you've wasted your time. But look at you. Your arms are strong and muscular. Your back is sinewy and tanned. Your hands are calloused from the constant pressure, and your legs have become stocky and firm. You have grown, and your abilities have increased a hundred-fold. You have been obedient. You trusted my wisdom. Now I will move the rock for you."

Sometimes we hear from the Lord, are obedient, and seemingly nothing happens. But all God wants from us is our obedience and our trust in Him.

The Preacher and the Atheist

A preacher and an atheist hairdresser once walked together through the slums of the city.

And the barber said to the preacher, "This is why I cannot believe in a God of love. If God was as loving as you claim, he would not allow all this poverty and all the diseases and misery. He would not allow these poor creatures to be addicted to drugs or other habits that destroy their character. No, I cannot believe in a God who allows these things."

The preacher remained silent until they met a man who looked exceptionally unkempt and dirty. His hair hung down over his face, greasy and uncombed, and he had not shaved for a long time.

Then the preacher said, "You can't be a very good hairdresser, or you wouldn't let a man in your neighborhood go without a decent haircut and shave."

The hairdresser replied indignantly, "How can you blame me for this man's condition? I can't help the way he looks. He's never come into my shop before. If he did, I could work on him and make him look like a gentleman."

The preacher looked at the barber with penetrating eyes and said, "Then don't blame God if people stay on their evil ways even though he constantly invites them to come to him and be redeemed.

Our Old Town When Times Were Bad and Money Scarce

Not so long ago in one city, the following happened. Times were bad and money scarce, they kept their families together with love as best they could, but the economy was down. The government made only promises, the banks remained closed, and almost everyone lived on credit from private donors.

The government advised people to look for new, modern jobs, and make a change, so to speak.

An unknown man from the community, a former commercial traveler tried his way. He booked a room for a whole week on the top floor of a restaurant and put down $500 as a deposit.

The restaurant owner immediately ran to the butcher with the banknote to pay off old debts. The latter promptly knocked on the baker's door to give him his borrowed 200 dollars back.

The baker dusted the flour off his apron and looked for the flour dealer to pay his outstanding bill.

The flour dealer took the money to the farmer and paid him for the grain he owed him from the previous year.

The farmer spied on his wife and quickly took the money, to pay the landlord his outstanding bill at the local pub and to have another beer.

The landlord immediately paid his debt to a beverage supplier who rushed off to pay the note to a cooperative investor.

The latter passed the money onto a lady with whom he was on credit. The lady, in turn, visited the restaurant owner, where she booked her room that was up for grabs at $100.

A few hours later, the former commercial traveler changed his mind and left the room. The restaurant owner, smiling, handed back his security deposit.

Thus nine people paid off their debts within a few hours and were able to start the new week in a happy mood.

But some residents of the community heard the story very differently. There was no money, the government made only promises, the banks remained closed, and as in the old days, people were left to their own destinies.

God's Wonderful Way

The True Story of the Evangelist Richard Baxter

The Evangelist Richard Baxter (1615 - 1691) had announced in a remote place in England an officially not allowed meeting for the proclamation of the Gospel at a very early morning hour. In order not to be late, he decided to ride to the place the evening before.

The night was dark. He got lost and finally knocked on the door of a nice house to ask for the way. A servant reported the stranger to his master. It seemed inappropriate to him that a man of such respectable appearance should wander about so late, so he invited him to stay with him for the night.

During their conversation, the host gained an even higher opinion of the intellect and erudition of his guest. He became eager to learn more about him and inquired about Tisch's profession.

Smiling, Baxter replied, "I am a people catcher."

"A man-catcher are you?" the landowner said, "well, you're just in time. You're just the man I need. I 'm the justice of the peace of this district, and I have been instructed to arrest a person named Richard Baxter, who is expected in the neighborhood tomorrow morning to hold a meeting.

Baxter agreed, and they rode to the appointed place the following day. When they arrived, a considerable number of people were already waiting near the house where the meeting was to be held. But as soon as the people saw the Lord of Justice, they became suspicious and did not dare to enter the house.

The judge finally said to his companion, "I suspect Baxter will have got wind of my order and will not show himself. I suggest we ride on ahead of for the time being, to keep the people safe."

But when they returned, the people still hesitated to go inside.

The Justice of the Peace assumed that the matter was unsuccessful and said to Baxter, "I would be much obliged if you would give a speech to these people to urge them to be loyal to the authorities."

Baxter replied, "Since the people have gathered to hold a service, such a speech would not serve them. But if you, Justice of the Peace, would like to begin with a prayer, I will see what more can be said."

"Oh," the judge replied, embarrassed, "I don't have a prayer book with me, otherwise, I would be happy to take up your suggestion. However, I am convinced that my honored guest is capable of both praying with the people and talking to them. I would ask you to do both at your discretion."

What could Baxter wish for more! They went into the house, and the crowd followed. Baxter prayed with such fervor that the judge standing next to him had tears in his eyes. And then he preached with great courage of faith. When he finished, he identified himself to the magistrate as the one he was going to arrest.

However, the judge had received a deep impression of the divine truth during the lecture. He later became a sincere Christian and at the same time a friend and advocate of the persecuted.

I Met Her in the Opera

As an old opera fan, I could only travel to New York in December. Even before I started my trip, I knew that December would be one of the coldest months in years, and days of snow had been forecast. My favorite opera singer would be performing at the Metropolitan Opera, so whatever the weather conditions were I was adamant about going on the cultural trip.

I was not planning to go just for the opera performance; culture was also on the agenda during the week. As a tourist, I had nothing better to do than to head to the Metropolitan Opera in the evening to buy tickets. At the box office, I could get a good seat. Not cheap. But with 199 dollars to burn, I took my chances. It was supposed to be the best seat in the stalls. Before purchasing the ticket, I had some time to look around in the Met gift shop, where you can buy beautiful jewelry under a hundred bucks as well as featured CDs.

Today they were showing *Porgy and Bess*, set amid a fictional African-American tenement, where love and friendship are tampered by addiction and violence. I thought that might be fitting in these strange times I have experienced lately anyway.

I asked the young saleswoman, who had a friendly expression if I had made a good choice.

"Yes," she said vividly, "I can certainly recommend it, all the performers are excellent."

I looked into the animated face with the big brown eyes, and without thinking, I said, "Are you a singer too?"

"Yes. How did you guess?"

"I just guessed." I shrugged my shoulders.

The young woman made the credit card booking. I let her work in peace. When the transaction was over, and I had signed, I picked up the thread of the conversation. "Well, If you don't mind me asking, what do you sing?"

"Oh, I'm just a soprano. And I've just finished my vocal studies."

"That's great. And now you sing at the MET?"

"Not yet. Maybe one day."

"Why not yet?"

"I guess my voice is too young for the MET. I'm only 25. It'll take me at least six more years to develop my voice enough to go to the big opera house."

"And you have to practice a lot?"

"Three hours a day. That's the norm. Every day."

I nodded approvingly. "I admire you!" And received an enchanting smile in return.

Casually I looked at the name tag of the young woman, Chermaine B. She noticed me looking.

"Just wondering, do you think there is an issue with Porgy and Bets, I mean have you read a lot about the controversies?"

She raised her eyebrows. "I can tell you this, I'm from Charleston in South Carolina, and at first I didn't like it at all. And now let me ask you. You're obviously not from here. Have you studied the background story?"

I felt heat creeping up my neck. I had been busted. "I am sorry. I haven't," I admitted.

"So I thought," she shook her head slightly, "Anyway, I think most customers don't know about it."

"Lots of people could have differences about the content," I said in a pleasant voice.

"She nodded. "That's probably true, especially since you're not from around here."

"I'm definitely not from this country that I can tell you."

"What country are you from?"

"Actually I'm German. However, I grew up in the UK.

"And I studied music in Vienna," she shot back with a smile.

"Unbelievable! Do you speak German?"

She laughed. "A little. I've been to Germany as well," she said in perfect High German.

I replied in German, "That's wonderful."

When it was time to leave. In English, I wished the young woman all the best for her future career. I predicted that she would be singing in the MET in just a few years and that I would then be desperately looking for a ticket to her performance.

She laughed again, and while I was studying the receipt to see if I could ask her more questions, she suddenly slipped me a note.

It read, *Next time we meet we can continue to talk about our points in common, not our differences.* At the bottom, she had added her phone number.

The Painter

Sunday mornings in New York are incomparable. The whole city is dedicated either to sports or to leisure, which in this city is mainly associated with music. Between these two opposites, there are few alternatives on a Sunday morning in Manhattan. And today I had a lot on my mind.

First, I took a taxi from the hotel to Battery Park. From there, I made my way through strollers and joggers, and young people on roller-blades, until I got to the dock where the ferryboat to the Statue of Liberty leaves. Later, after visiting Lady Liberty and Ellis Island, I returned to Battery Park.

There was a loud noise coming from one part of the park. A rock band was practising for an afternoon concert. I turned to the quieter part of the park, from where I could once again enjoy a beautiful view of the

Statue of Liberty in the distance, which was bathed in sunlight.

I took my last photo. Then the film was over. I tore myself away from the view and walked through the park, towards the city. My goal was to find a taxi to Soho.

Then on my left, on a quiet path, I noticed a painter standing in front of his easel. Sometimes he looked into the trees, which were visible in all details under the deep blue sky, sometimes he gave his already advanced work a brushstroke. When I got up close to the artist, I also noticed his paint box, in which all the oil paints were neatly lined up. The palette, which he held in his left hand, was full of spots of color. A picture rose before me.

I had taken painting lessons from a talented artist ten years ago in my hometown. At that time, I had also owned an easel, a canvas and paints. Unfortunately, I had given up this hobby because I had gone abroad. I watched the painter at work for a few moments without saying anything and studied the painting.

In the foreground, it had the path, then came the trees full of green foliage, and in the back right one could make out the outline of a modern black high-rise building. That is how it looked in reality. The light-flooded, impressionistic painting seemed to me to be quite successful, only the high-rise building in the background seemed out of place.

I voiced my observation to the artist, who looked at me amused under his bushy eyebrows. A middle-aged man with a peculiar long-groomed mustache, just like your stereotype artists. And a genre painter.

"Yes, you're right," he replied. "I think I'll paint over that tower block eventually. It actually bothers me."

"But it's already done in dark colors," I dared to say.

"Right, and I'll get rid of it." He kept on painting a tree.

"A long time ago, I too painted," I interrupted. "Too bad I don't do it anymore. In '89 I picked it up again."

"You will probably laugh," replied the artist. "I don't feel much different. The last time I painted was twenty-five years ago. "I've only recently started painting again."

I nodded approvingly.

"But you know," he went on, after he had applied another brushstroke, and looked at the painting examining it, "there is a problem."

"What's that?" I asked.

"You've got to be damn careful this hobby doesn't turn into work if you spend too much time on it."

I nodded seriously. "I can relate to that, I feel the same way, but in a different area. I write as a hobby, and I have a tendency to invest too much time and energy in it. There is also a risk that my hobby will suddenly become my work, which would be a pity."

"That's exactly how it is," the man replied, "hobby and work should be separated. Otherwise, both will suffer in the end. And above all, a hobby must not become work, because all the fun might end."

"And how do you do that? I mean, where do you draw the line ?"

He looked up to me, somewhat surprised. "Sometimes I ask for guidance, like with so many other affairs, you understand?"

For a second, I looked sideways. "Not really. Whom do you ask for guidance."

He smiled and pointed a finger to the sky. "To someone greater than me. "

I nodded again in agreement. "Yes, I think I understand..." Then I said a heartfelt goodbye to the hobby artist.

On my way home, I was thinking of his words and message. Even though it was such a trivial matter, the man had reminded me of something that I had almost forgotten.

Cafe Lisbon

In September last year, I was in Washington with my friend Fritz. He's the kind of person who's always in a good mood. I have never seen Fritz sad or depressed. He succeeds in everything in life. It's nice that there are such people!

One evening we went out for dinner in a small restaurant next to a Casino mall. What was served was excellent. After dessert, I ordered a coffee and a French cognac, all European. As we sat outside, I was overcome by the desire for a cigar.

"Do you have any?" I asked, the restaurant's Chinese manager.

"No, unfortunately, not," was his answer. "We'd be hanged," he said with a sense of humor. "But I know a bar nearby where they have cigars—the Cafe Lisbon. Go out here, then turn left, then right at the next intersection and then left again on the next street. There you'll find Cafe Lisbon. You can't miss it."

I thanked him for the good advice. We paid and left. We found Cafe Lisbon without a problem. The directions given by the restaurant owner had been correct.

At the entrance of the well-kept place, which was open to the outside on this warm September night, we were welcomed by a European-looking patron. He gave us a winning smile as if we were his very best old friends.

"Erminio is my name. And what is yours?"

"I am Paul. My friend's name is Fritz," I told him. "Do you have cigars?"

"Yes, of course! Lots of cigars. Cubans and others. Would you like a Montecristo?"

"Yes, I would. Number four, please."

"You got it, boss," was his answer. "Head to the bar now. You'll find what you're looking for."

The bar was long and crowded. We could hardly find a gap to reach the bar. Soon our two cigars were there waiting for us there. I ordered another coffee and cognac. Fritz took a beer. Soon I was alone at a small bar table, from where I could watch the whole restaurant. Straight ahead of me was the bar, behind me the actual restaurant. Some people were still eating, although it was already half-past ten in the evening.

Where was Fritz? He had gone to the toilet. But where was he now? To my astonishment, I saw him standing at the bar with a blond lady. He toasted with her. Then he kissed her on the cheeks, and very gently, on the mouth. I couldn't believe my eyes. Next to him stood a man of about fifty-seven who seemed to be with the blond woman but hardly took any notice of what Fritz was doing. *Other countries, other customs,* I thought to myself.

Opposite me was an Englishman holding court, who must have been in his forties or fifties. He drank one beer after the other and saluted me from afar. I left my bar table and walked towards him. I cheered to him, the big pot-bellied brandy glass in my hand.

"What are you doing here in Washington?" he asked me. "Politics?" Washington is full of politicians and lobbyists.

"No. I'm European. I'm here on a visit."

"That's good," nodded the Englishman. "We need friendship between the Old and New Continents. Do you like the women here?"

The stranger squeezed a young or young-at-heart woman, pale, blond and blue-eyed, who looked like a living copy of Marilyn Monroe. "By the way, this is Jane. And this gentleman is a European, who hasn't told me his name yet."

"Delighted," I said to Jane and shook her hand. Then I also shook hands with the Englishman. "My name is Paul. What is your name?"

"Well, it's a bit complicated," said the stranger. "I am the son of an English lord. If that's enough for you. Call me Harry that will do. I'm here to build a racetrack for Formula One in Las Vegas. Big thing." He took another sip of beer. "But forget all that. The only thing that matters in this goddamn world is women. Women like Jane." He pressed the beautiful one to himself again, who put up with his strong embrace, not looking as though she liked it, or maybe just didn't care.

Then I returned to my little table. I longed for a sip of coffee. As time passed, the place emptied. Fritz was not quite aware that flirting can be a double-edged sword in America. Anyone who knew him would know that he didn't care anyway. In the meantime, he had already made a pass at a Latino beauty who had round, dark eyes and looked very different. She was also well dressed. Soon he was sitting at a table with her and waved me over. I sat down there as well.

"This is my friend Pablo," he introduced me. "And this is Juanita from Mexico who works here in Washington."

I shook hands with the young woman and exchanged a few words with her. But then quite unexpectedly, Juanita turned back to Fritz.

There as a blond gentleman in his fifties at our table who stood out because of his peach-red jacket. The man looked incredibly sad and tired as if he was about to die. 'Tired of life' crossed my mind. I introduced myself to the man.

"My name is Hans," he answered. "Hans from Sweden." He paused. "I have a house here in Washington. I have several houses in Sweden. I have a house in Gstaad. I have houses everywhere."

"That's wonderful," I answered.

"That's what you think," was his answer. "But houses, like women, only cause problems."

He looked at Jane, who had now come to our table. She had finally broken away from Harry, the English lord's son.

Hans pointed at Jane with an eerily tired gesture. "Do you see this wonderful young woman? I love her. But she wants nothing to do with me. That's a pity."

Jane patted his hand. She looked at him with a perfect Marilyn Monroe smile, coupled with an eerily sharp look. "Nonsense darling. Of course, I love you too. I love you a lot. But in a different way. Understand that!"

Hans sighed, took a long sip from his whisky glass and turned back to me. "You see, this is how a cruel woman speaks. She wants nothing to do with me but loves me anyway. Have you ever understood how a woman works?"

Jane had heard all this but kept looking at him with a sweet smile that was as clear as a still, pure lake.

"Of course women are different from men," I now tried to comfort Hans, "but there must be some way you can get along with Jane."

"If only I could find it," sighed Hans and turned back to his whisky glass.

Jane and Juanita said goodbye. They were going to another bar. Hans waved goodbye. He was too tired to do anything more. Jane voiced a tender farewell to Hans and he received an enchanting smile and a big kiss on the cheek. *That's the way Marilyn must have kissed*, I thought. Hans was now no longer responsive. I said goodbye to him. Together with Fritz, I went back to the hotel.

The London Marathon

It was by chance that I was in London last April. It was the last Sunday of the month when the marathon is traditionally held, attracting tens of thousands of participants and spectators. I was in the second category. Together with my Swiss friend, I went to the end of the small park in Blackheath in the morning around eleven o'clock, where the numerous Swiss runners had set up their so-called Swiss Curve.

The charming lady at the Swiss Consulate General in London immediately gave me a red and white T-shirt with a large Swiss cross in the middle. Unfortunately, I was too late for the distribution of the racy caps with the Swiss colors, which was not tragic, as the day was mild and beautiful, and the sun was not burning down on us.

The over thirty thousand runners had already started at ten o'clock to cover the distance of over 42 kilometers.

Our Swiss place on the marathon course was at kilometer 33. Not very far from the finish line, which would finally bring salvation to the runners, after crossing the Embankment to Parliament Square. This meant that we could only expect to see the runners by the beginning of the afternoon. On a small table, we offered glasses with coke and fruit. We wanted to offer the runners, especially the Swiss contingent, some refreshments when they arrived at some point.

I passed the time talking to Swiss people who lived in London. I soon realized that I was dealing with a large number of very successful businessmen who loved London and Switzerland equally, and who had one thing above all else, success in life. That's what life is all about in the end.

Next to the Swiss stand, a big band from Barbados and Tobago had settled down, chasing hot rhythms into the deep blue late autumn day, which was still part of the Indian Summer. The boys and girls created terrific sounds from the oil barrels. Eventually, they danced to the music, giving rise to a small carnival.

Finally, there was movement on the previously empty street. Police cars and publicity trucks drove by. A camera team filmed the spectators. The Mayor of London drove by in a classic open vehicle. People cheered.

At last, the first runner came into view, then others, first only a handful, then suddenly a large mass. The Swiss Embassy ran past, accompanied by a small bodyguard proudly carrying a Swiss flag.

We were suddenly very busy at the stand. I was cutting bananas, and another Swiss guy kept on refilling coke while his colleague put new cups on the table. Our customers were by no means all Swiss. But that didn't matter at all.

The main thing was that we were of service to these hungry and thirsty runners, which was gratefully acknowledged. There was already some publicity for Switzerland, as some colleagues from the Consulate General busily waved Swiss flags and rang cowbells. Those who kept their eyes closed could truly imagine themselves in the Swiss Alps. We were in Harlem, where it was teeming with black children who enthusiastically wore Swiss T-shirts and red and white caps.

Sometime between three and four o'clock in the afternoon, the race came to an end. There were now only a few isolated runners who were simply walking as they would on a Sunday walk. But many looked terrible, sweaty and exhausted. Pity was stirring in me. The things that man does to himself!

I spotted an old, thin woman who really looked like a mummy — only skin and bones, but I quickly realized she was a marathon runner because of her sports shoes and T-shirt. She was totally exhausted. Suddenly she came right up and looked at me with a strange but gentle expression. Wordlessly I gave her coke and banana chips. I swallowed at the sight of her and cleared my throat.

"I admire you."

Her old eyes flashed, suddenly she seemed to awaken. "Are you sure about that?" she asked.

"Well, let me ask you, why are you doing this Marathon?"

"To show and prove faith."

I shook my head slightly. "At your age, you don't need to prove anything."

She took one step closer, then pointed her finger at the sky.

"No for me, for Him." She nodded at me again, then slowly walked down the empty street.

Later, I returned with my friend to the house where he lived, where I had rented a room next door. We said goodbye.

"Will we see you again next year at Swiss Curve at the London Marathon? I'd be delighted."

"I'll let you know later," I answered somewhat sheepishly.

A few months later, my friend called again. "So, I'll see you next April in London at the marathon?"

"Yes, and I'm going to compete," I replied proudly.

"You want to run. Are you sure?"

"Absolutely."

He paused on the phone for several seconds. "May I ask you why you're doing this?"

"I'm doing it for HIM, because of my faith, my friend."

Endless Love on a Dream Vacation

For many weeks I had been looking forward to our summer holiday back in the old country, in Italy. But unlike most of my family, I have a completely different emotional connection to my country of origin — anyway, five whole days off! We had never had such long holidays before! We wanted to go to Northern Italy and drive around by car. There was a special occasion to drive through this region, but it doesn't play a role in my memories.

In the end, it became a hectic journey as we drove from city to city along the Riviera, only staying everywhere for a few hours.

This strange and stressful journey was intensified by a sort of inner conflict of which I want to tell you about.

It was a dream and conflict at the same time. I was sitting on a rock on an ocean shore and felt the unquenchable longing for the sea. The feverish expectation to smell the waves, to taste them, to grasp them, to meet with them, to greet the wind! Oh, I had not been home for so long, so long!

For what could have been a few seconds or eternity, I felt I belonged to the sea, and had been driven from there by terrible fate. In reality, I had seen the sea for the first time when I was twenty-seven!

To me, the sea was much more than a big, moving bathtub. Much more than something to enjoy or not, like other people think about mountains or deserts.

To feel the proximity of the sea and tremble every minute — to feel it, to greet it, to talk to it, to play with it, to laugh — all connected with strange sensations, as if the long separation from a loved one was finally over. I felt my love for this sea was endless, or so I thought.

These were the sensations that made a carefree stay in beautiful Italy impossible.

Where did this pulling in the heart come from?

It was a strange bondage, which I continued to suffer through during the first night in my home bed as powerfully and painfully as never before. How I had tried to catch a glimpse of the beach, of the glistening green and blue surface from every viewpoint on the Autostrada!

Why did I have to leave MY sea again? I rolled from one side to the other and could not cope with it.

Suddenly, I felt someone was looking over me. Eyes full of love and sadness. Whose eyes? It suddenly became clear to me. Someone or something was there who had more claim to my love than this wet element, the sea. It was someone who for my sake, had left the glory of heaven and given up his precious life offering this indestructible life to me.

It was his eyes that asked me, "Do you prefer my creature, the sea, which can never return your feelings? Have you ever experienced when it stands up as a mortal enemy against man and the water brings ruin without pity? Will you chain yourself to it as if it were your own dearest?"

Boy, oh boy, how ashamed I was that night! How could I ever forget?

The sea is not taken away from me — no, it is only a shackle torn. The bond almost chafed my heart.

I can now stand freely at the edge of the waves, admiring the broad, golden band with inner jubilation.

My Name is Lazarus - A Classic Tale

What is there special to tell you about me? I was one of the most insignificant people who ever lived under the sun of the Almighty. If a book in which the stories of all those who once lived were written, two lines would satisfy the demand to describe my life. Indeed, I have always believed in God somewhere, but in my past, even that was rather superficial.

I endured my suffering with patience, as best I could. What else could I do? Even if everything was taken away from me and everything was granted me, I still had hope for something better. Not in this world, but in a future one, I thought, and right I should be.

My life was only a cold breeze from which one would like to be protected, a passing dark cloud in the otherwise so bright blue sky. Most days were filled with pain, suffering and sorrow. I had long since given up hope of recovery, but the worst thing for me was contempt. They looked down on me and turned away again. Or they pretended that I did not exist and continued to talk to each other in their seemingly important disputes about politics, finance, profits, and maintaining the value of life.

I admit, my sight must have been shocking to those who were well-off in their silk and fine thread. Their large bellies covered with cloaks and cleansed feet encased in the finest leather, that merely touched the ground let alone poverty.

For weeks now, I had been lying here in front of the great, mighty wrought-iron gate of that noble, respected gentleman's castle — that is what I would call it if it were mine. He passed by me day in, day out, his head held high, on his way to important business deals, trade deals and contracts.

I looked up at him with one eye only, the other blinded and purulent, and picked up the scent of prosperity, satisfaction and self-satisfaction. My hair, which had not been cut for a long time, stuck to my cheeks and neck, had become a dwelling to numerous small lodgers, who fed on my scales and made me itch, but I have long since stopped complaining about fleas. My clothes were tattered and did not sufficiently cover the bruised, ulcer-ridden body. Why do the dogs find such pleasure in licking ulcers after sniffing their own excrement? The smell must be the same. It was as if I was already a rotten carrion, or did they think with their God-given innocence, they could give me pleasure and relief with a wet, cool tongue. If this is how it was, they are forgiven for having helped my wounds through greater pain with their organ contaminated by rubbish.

The noble gentleman, however, did not look at me, and his feet never touched mine when he passed or had to step over me.

On some days, when plagues tore at my limbs or hunger drove me into a doldrums, I made it difficult for him to ignore me. Still, he always managed to make a face of humiliation and to show me my worthlessness. What is my fault? What did I want from him? Only the right to be left to live, the least in this world. I did not think of reveling in high spirits and full splendor. I only wanted enough to survive with.

From time to time, the maid from his kitchen would sneak past me. She was pretty in the apron she wore and with the grace she possessed. She turned the corner of the house and saw me there. Her smile wanted to give me mercy, but her eyes betrayed horror. She moved around several sides, then she knelt down to give me the leftovers that the noble gentleman had spurned after over-satiation and wanted to remember the dogs.

But the maid was charitable and left me some edible leftovers. However, I was never alone, for the dogs also hung on to life and wagged their tails when they saw the maid.

So the days and the nights, the weeks and the months passed, and the last winter of my life is now a while behind me. My memory is still clear, though without grudge or charge.

Shortly after, the maid herself fell seriously ill, she brought me a large ration of food that was still warm. She put an old blanket, which belonged to her, around my emaciated shoulders and thought of me with all the warmth she was able to give me. She never spoke a word, but I understood her nevertheless, and read through the window of her kind eyes, the message of love and grace that the Almighty is ready to give at a time we do not know, on a path we do not choose.

On that day, I saw her for the last time and apart from the blanket and her goodness, nothing else was able to prolong my earthly life.

I often wondered during many hours how it would be to leave this world and travel to another, but I had no choice than to wait, consumed by the hope for better things and encouraged by the goodness of this maid.

The day of my journey began with a silent cry. I could only vaguely distinguish it, as my senses were dwindling, and my heart was pricked in my chest. But as I leaned up towards heaven one last time, a great, powerful angel stood before my humble camp. He shone brighter than the sun, and his wings measured more cubits than the birds of primeval times. Everything about him was extraordinary, but not frightening. His gaze reminded me of the way the maid had looked at me, with compassion and goodness. For a moment, I felt as if she stood before me transformed. He bent over me without disgust or fear and effortlessly took me in his strong arms, as one would hold a small child. I looked around and saw my body lying there. I felt naked and unclothed in view of the ragged wrappings I had left there, certainly not to the joy of the noble Lord. I became aware that I still existed, even without pain and without plagues. It seemed as if the dogs were laughing, for they looked up to me in their own eagerness for redemption, wagging their shaggy tails joyfully, and watching us gradually disappear from their sight.

"Rest in peace," people say when they put a body in the pit, but they do not know what true rest means. In the arm of my angel, I sensed that I would be part of this rest.

"Where are you taking me?" I asked the angel.

"To the dwelling place of the righteous of God, where you shall find comfort for the shame you have suffered," he spoke into my consciousness, although his lips did not move.

"How is it possible that I'm still here, that I talk to you and feel safe in your arms?"

"You have merely unclothed yourself, Lazarus, but the place assigned to you cannot be found without me. Your existence has no end, and the dress can be changed. The breath of the Supreme still fills your soul, your mind and your intellect, for these are eternal, just as the Supreme is. The time will come when you will have a new garment, an imperishable and expensive one, bought at a high price, together with those who call justice their inheritance. But now we are in the place of his choice, where consolation and forgetfulness will accompany you until the day when the trumpet sounds and you are given an eternal abode."

Gently he set me down, although I could have easily jumped down. I felt splendid and light, elated and freed from all the burdens of my bruised and starved body. One last time the angel gave me a look full of love and mercy and filled my hungry heart. Then he was no longer to be seen, and I was alone.

I looked around and found a place that I had never dreamed of even in my most beautiful dreams. I also lack the words to describe this place of peace adequately, as there is no such place on our earth.

I was not alone, nor was it dark or hot, but bright and pleasantly warm. A strange light prevailed, and I could not make out the source of the light.

I discovered Abraham, who was pleased to see me. He, the model of my faith, stood by me to comfort and ease my suffering. Not the sufferings of my body, but those of my heart, the contempt and shame that I had tasted in abundance during my lifetime.

"Where are we, father Abraham?" I asked him curiously, but without haste.

"This is the place of the unclothed righteous, the place of our rest. In earlier times it was called Sheol, but in more recent writings it is written as Hades. It is equal to paradise, for all that a man needs for survival can be found here."

"How long will we have to stay here?"

"The time of our resurrection is not known to me either, but you will not feel hours, days or years here. The experience of time is tied to transience, this place is imperishable. On Earth, we measure time by the fulfillment of our wishes and the achievement of new goals. Here, however, is a place of rest, of waiting, and for us, who have been justly spoken of by the Father of Life, it is a place of comfort and peace."

"What happens to other people who do evil and spurn God's love and grace?" I asked Abraham and leaned against him.

At that moment, we heard a loud, desperate voice coming from far away. I looked in the direction of the sound and could see a human being standing there, wrapped in bright light, yes it could have been fire, but the flames did not engulf him. It seemed as if they were just playing with him and making him feel the heat. Except for the light of this fire, it was pitch dark there and oppression emanated from the place. I discovered many other people over there, they were all alone, complaining, whimpering and without hope.

"What does this man call to you, Abraham? Do you know him, and how does he know you?" I asked the man on whose shoulder I was leaning.

"This man you see and hear is that noble Lord at whose gates you have waited in vain for compassion and mercy. He also died, but he was not carried to this place by the angels of the Lord. He longs to receive the relief that is denied him there. He suffers torment in his flame, and he beseeches that you dip your finger in freshwater to cool his tongue."

"Oh, *now* he notices me," I protested indignantly. "Before I was air for him, now I'm supposed to ease his pain?"

"You would do it, Lazarus, if it were possible, for you are of a different breed than he."

Abraham called out to the formerly rich and noble, now stripped, whining and miserable.

"It is not possible to send Lazarus to you, for we are separated by a deep and wide, insurmountable gorge, so that no one can change sides, however much he desires it," Abraham called to him. "Furthermore, remember that you have already received your share of good in your lifetime, but Lazarus only bad. Now he will be comforted for this, but you must suffer."

Full of despair, he answered him from a distance, "Then send him to my father's house and to my five brothers, that they too may not come to this place of torment."

"Your brothers can read in the Word of God given to them for instruction, they can hear Moses and the prophets," Abraham replied.

The voice of the tormented man became louder and louder and pleaded, "No, father Abraham, only when one of the dead comes to them will they repent."

Then Abraham said, "If they do not listen to Moses and the prophets, they will not be persuaded when one rises from the dead."

I watched this event with great interest. I was astonished that after death, as we called and suspected it, everything was quite different. I had not hated the rich man during his lifetime, and I did even less now. My heart was filled with the power of the inevitable, the unchangeable. No possibility of repentance would be open to this man, for the time of grace was over for him. I, however, fought all my earthly life with privations and in the end starved and froze to death in my body, but always in joyful expectation of this time and even more so of the future. If I am here now in the place of the stripped righteousness of God. The only justice that I am aware of within my miserable life is that I believed in a good God, in Christ, who already carried my shame by bleeding on the cross and who became justice for me.

One last time on this long day, although there is no such thing for me anymore, I turned to the Father of faith. "What could the noble Lord have done better to avoid coming to the place of torment? Would faith in Christ have saved him?"

Abraham answered, and I discovered kindness and sadness in his voice, "Yes, it would have. This would have changed his hard heart. His problem was not money and riches, but his selfishness toward people like you, as he chose not to share it and reduce your suffering."

Abraham rose and went on to comfort and heal the wounds of other deceased people, leaving me alone but not lonely for the time being.

There is still much to learn and to understand in this place and in the others that follow. Even if time no longer exists as a measure of my experience, I have — humanly speaking — enough of it. It will, however, not be long enough in the presence of my Redeemer.

Are We Alone in the Universe?

I never liked the hot weather in Florida. For twenty-one years, I have dreamed of traveling to Canada, this cool, friendly country in the north. Right after my birthday, I bought the cheapest ticket to a place that I was sure had to be better.

Now I am north of Halifax, but I cannot say that I feel comfortable here. All alone, here in the hotel, I feel as though I've been eradicated from a place, and as if I don't have all my senses.

Night falls, and I still lie awake in my bed. The window is wide open because it is a balmy summer night. The wind gently moves the leaves of the big old chestnut tree outside my window. It is as if the old giant is dreaming of times gone by as it gently sways its densely leafy branches back and forth. Softly it rustles and sounds through the silent warm night, and the big round moon breaks out between the branches of the old tree like a silver disc. The delicate play of sounds hanging in the branches of the chestnut tree conjures up the most wonderful tones.

The curtains in front of my window billow in the warm breeze, and from a distance, a lonely nightingale sings its song.

Silently I get up, to stand by the open window and look up at the starry sky. The night is so wonderfully clear. The tent of stars looks like thousands of glittering diamonds on a deep blue velvet blanket.

Many people ask themselves, "Are we alone in the universe? Is there something beyond our imagination? Who did all this? What comes next? Are we really alone?"

No, I don't think so! The Bible already tells us that nothing is left to chance here, and behind all this beauty, an eternal creator stands and works.

When I look at the starry firmament, I automatically remember that biblical passage from the book of JOB which says that the angels before God's throne are called 'morning stars'. That they all rejoiced together when they saw their Creator calling our world into being. The angels have their special tasks as servant spirits. They guard, protect, guide and comfort us, humans, in all situations of life. The cherubim have four wings, and the seraphim even have six, reports the Bible. I desire to see such a wonderful messenger more than anything else.

Perhaps there is also an 'angel of the night', I think to myself.

Such a night angel sits quietly by the beds of the children, consoles the lonely and sick, dries hot tears and puts his mighty, strong arm around them.

Silently I sneak back into my bed so as not to disturb the nightingale's beautiful night song, imagining it can hear me.

Once again, I recall the last minutes and my eyelids become heavy. The soft sound of the wind in the tree, the rustling of the leaves, the aria of the nightingale and the gentle whispering of the wind gradually cradle me into a peaceful deep slumber.

No! We are not alone in the universe! There are angels of God around us, and they are powerful helpers who will one day guard our grave and be the first to greet us on the resurrection morning. Then there will no longer be a dividing line between this world and the world beyond. Oh, if only it were already morning!

Different Heavens According to Peter

For hours I had knocked and begged loudly until the heavenly door finally opened with a squeak. I stepped over the threshold and found myself at the entrance of a long, white corridor. The corridor led up to a stairway. On every other step, a set of doors stood opposite one another to the right and left as if guarding the passageway.

"Is this the way to the gateway, or is it the corridor to the great heaven?" I asked Peter.

"No," he said, "this is simply the ordinary Christian heaven."

"So, only a Christian heaven? Is there any other heaven?" I asked the former fisherman from the Sea of Galilee.

"But of course there is," replied Peter, "there is still the human heaven. It's actually a festive hall, with music and an eternal buffet."

Peter pointed with his right hand to the very sterile-looking corridor.

"See, the first door on the right is for the Catholics. The one opposite is for the Gospels. Then come the Baptists, the Methodists, Adventists, Mennonites and so on. There is a room for traditional and conservative Christians, for liberals and for charismatics, for the Bible believers and the fundamentalists. There is a door for each denomination. But believe me, every one of these rooms is terribly boring! Everyone agrees with each other. No one discusses anything at all. People simply nod their heads, pat each other on the back, and nothing more is said about the subject. Oh, and by the way, the corridor is eight light minutes long."

I knew that this was the exact distance from the sun to our planet. Unbelievable.

"At the end of the corridor on the right," Peter continued, "is the office of John the Baptist. He explains the Old and New Testaments to the highly educated theologians and eternal sages."

I was rather flattered and asked him, whom he thought should have been the first pope.

"Who is in the real heaven, the human heaven. Are there also Muslims and so on?"

"Of course there are," the fisherman replied. "There are also Jews, non-denominational, non-religious, Buddhists, Hindus, free thinkers, agnostics and atheists, prostitutes, homosexuals and even a few Christians."

"And who opens the door to heaven?"

Peter smiled at me and whispered, "You will not believe it. Three of them take it in turns. Mahatma Gandhi, Martin Luther King and Nelson Mandela. For

Jesus has decided that only those who give and grant freedom to others are true men and true Christians. It even says so in the Bible — if you read carefully enough."

I was stunned. I really hadn't expected that. I had been thinking more along the lines of the Archangel Gabriel and his colleagues, or Mary and Joseph or those akin. I had one last question for Peter.

"Is there any possibility for me to get from here to the human, the real heaven? And why am I here in the first place, in this seemingly barren heaven?"

"Well," said Peter, "like you, everyone comes through here at first. And I ask each one question. Now, depending on their answer, the person either stays here or is allowed to go to heaven, which, by the way, really deserves its name."

I started to shiver. What question Peter would ask me? One from the Old Testament, or the New? Was this some sort of Bible quiz?

Peter put his hand on my left shoulder and looked at me, his eyes filled with kindness. "Just relax. You'll find the answer. But before I ask the question, I would like to inform you and also remind you of the following — Your planet Earth is a speck of dust in the overall picture of the universe. Neptune, at the edge of your solar system, is 4.1 light-hours — one light-second equals 300,000 earthly kilometers away from the sun. The nearest star, Alpha,

is 4.36 light-years from your solar system. Your galaxy, with a diameter of 100,000 light-years, has another 100 to 300 billion stars and suns. The entire universe, however, consists of at least another 100 billion galaxies, each with several hundred billion suns. The galaxy closest to you begins at a distance of 2.5 million light-years, and you named it Andromeda. The age of the universe known to you is 13.819 billion years, and it has a diameter of 93 billion light-years. It is known that the universe is still expanding and — who would have thought it — there are other universes as well."

Peter paused, took a deep breath and then he finally asked the dreaded question, "Tell me who, how and what is GOD, you speck of dust upon another speck of dust, the Earth. Do you really think you can answer this question?"

Now this question was also on Peter's mind. I remember how I answered spontaneously, and I did not ponder on whether the answer would block the longed-for path to eternity.

"No, Lord," I said, "no, I don't know."

Peter smiled broadly, and I sighed, relieved. "Come," he said, "I will show you the way to paradise."

I was suddenly overwhelmed by audacity, and, with a wink in my earthly eye, I asked the fisherman, "Does Jesus still turn water into wine there?"

Peter laughed out loud and said, "Sure, of course, and of the best quality. It wouldn't be heaven otherwise, would it?"

***

Details of all the author's available books and upcoming titles can be found at:

www.shortstoycollections.com

www.ingramcontent.com/pod-product-compliance
Lightning Source LLC
Chambersburg PA
CBHW021146080526
44588CB00008B/235